Inspecting Schools for Race Equality:
OFSTED's Strengths and Weaknesses
A Report for the Commission for Racial Equality

Audrey Osler and Marlene Morrison

A report for the Commission for Racial Equality
published by Trentham Books

First published in 2000 by Trentham Books Limited

Trentham Books Limited
Westview House
734 London Road
Oakhill
Stoke on Trent
Staffordshire
England ST4 5NP

British Cataloguing in Publication Data
A catalogue record for this book is available from the British Library
ISBN 1 85856 235 X

Designed and typeset by Trentham Print Design Ltd., Chester and
printed in Great Britain by Cromwell Press Ltd., Wiltshire.

CONTENTS

Acknowledgements • viii
Acronyms and Abbreviations • ix
Foreword • xi

Executive Summary • xv
Introduction • xv
The current and previous inspection frameworks • xvii
HMI perspectives on race equality and school inspection • xviii
Inspectors' perspectives • xix
School inspection reports • xxi
Headteachers' perspectives • xxii
Recommendations • xxiii

Chapter 1
Introduction • 1
Structure of the report • 1
Aims and objectives of the research • 2
Evidence to demonstrate objectives • 3
Context • 4
Research design and methodology • 7

Chapter 2
The OFSTED inspection framework and race equality • 11
The context • 11
Macpherson and OFSTED's lead role in preventing racism • 12
Evidence from HMCI's Report 1998-99 to the Secretary
of State for Education • 13
OFSTED's formal response to Macpherson • 20
Educational inclusion and race equality • 21
The OFSTED inspection framework and race equality • 27
Conclusion • 38

Chapter 3

HMI perspectives on race equality and school inspection • 39

Inspection frameworks and race equality • 40

Educational inclusion • 49

Inspection processes • 52

Individuals' understandings of race equality in education • 55

The role of OFSTED in preventing racism through education • 58

Conclusion • 67

Chapter 4

Inspectors' perspectives • 69

At the cutting edge • 69

Frameworks to support the goals of race equality • 70

Ethnicity: pupil composition and school characteristics • 73

Curriculum issues • 75

Provision for pupils with English as an additional language • 76

Inspecting white schools • 77

Pupils' spiritual, moral, social and cultural development • 78

School leadership • 80

Relationships with parents and the community • 81

Failing schools • 82

Ways forward • 83

Chapter 5

School inspection reports • 87

Inspecting the 'inspectable'? • 87

The literature review • 88

Our approach to document analysis • 91

OFSTED documents • 92

Statistical data from schools • 95

Inspection team documents • 96

Analysis of published inspection reports • 102

What kind of school is this? • 103

What are the educational standards achieved? • 108

How good are the curriculum opportunities
offered to all pupils? • 111

To what extent does teaching meet the needs of pupils for whom
English is an additional language? • 114

How well do schools care for their pupils? • 117
Do reports present evidence on the effectiveness of a school's
partnership with parents and the community? • 120
Overview • 121
Conclusions • 124

Chapter 6
Headteachers' perspectives • 127
Race equality on the agenda? • 127
Ethnic monitoring, target setting and standards • 131
Inspecting English as an additional language • 135
White schools and race equality • 138
Race and the community • 140
Can race equality be inspected? • 143
The political context of inspection • 145
Summary • 146

Chapter 7
Conclusions and recommendations • 149
OFSTED and its responsibilities in preventing
and addressing racism • 149
Inspectors' perspectives • 150
Inspection reports • 152
Headteachers' perceptions • 153
Can race equality be inspected? • 153
Recommendations • 154

References • 157

Appendices
Appendix item 1 Interview Schedule: Inspectors • 161
Appendix item 2 Interview Schedule: Headteachers • 163
Appendix item 3 Correspondence between Audrey Osler
and HMCI, Chris Woodhead • 165
Appendix item 4 An Inspection Framework for Race Equality
and Social Justice • 169
Appendix item 5 OFSTED Judgement Recording
Form: School • 173
Appendix item 6 Text search in BRS data base • 179

Acknowledgements

We would like to thank a number of people for their contributions to this report. We are appreciative of the support and cooperation of OFSTED in carrying out the research and, in particular wish to thank David Read and Hiral Sheth who provided us with a range of documents and statistical information. We are grateful to all those who gave up their time to be interviewed: members of HMI, contracted inspectors, headteachers and LEA officers. Although it is not appropriate to name them here we wish to thank them all for sharing their experiences and insights with us. Thanks to Susie Parsons, Phil Barnett, Joe Charlesworth and Greville Percival at the Commission for Racial Equality. Thanks also to Susan Fryett and all those in the School of Education research office who assisted with the transcription of tapes and to Samantha Keenan for support with the editorial process. To Judith Lavender who provided the index at such short notice. We would also like to thank those loyal colleagues who have read various drafts of our work: Dr. Hugh Starkey, Dr. Rob Watling and Tom Whiteside. Also Dr Gillian Klein for enthusiasm and commitment to the project. Their support is much appreciated.

Audrey Osler and Marlene Morrison
July 2000

Authors

Professor Audrey Osler is Director of the Centre for Citizenship Studies in Education at the University of Leicester. Before taking up an academic career, she taught in both primary and secondary schools and worked as a member of the LEA advisory services.

Dr Marlene Morrison is a lecturer in education (Research Methods) and Deputy Director of the Centre for Citizenship Studies in Education. She teaches across a range for postgraduate and professional programmes at the School of Education.

ACRONYMS AND ABBREVIATIONS

CEPPP   Centre for Public Policy and Practice

CRE   Commission for Racial Equality

DfEE   Department for Education and Employment

EAL   English as an Additional Language

EMAG   Ethnic Minority Achievement Grant

EMTAG   Ethnic Minority and Traveller Achievement Grant

EO   Equal Opportunities

GCSE   General Certificate of Secondary Education

HMCI   Her Majesty's Chief Inspector of Schools

HMI   Her Majesty's Inspector/Inspectorate

LEA   Local Education Authority

OFSTED   Office for Standards in Education

PSHE   Personal, Social and Health Education

PICSI   Pre-Inspection Context and School Indicator (a report prepared by an OFSTED Registered Inspector in preparation for a school inspection)

QCA   Qualifications and Curriculum Authority

RE   Religious Education

Regi   OFSTED Registered Inspector – a common shorthand used by headteachers and contracted inspectors

RGI   OFSTED Registered Inspector

Section 10 reports   OFSTED school inspection reports

SEN   Special Educational Needs

SMSC   Spiritual, Moral, Social and Cultural Development

SMT   Senior Management Team

Update   An OFSTED publication directed to contracted inspectors. Recent editions are available on the OFSTED website.

x

Foreword

GURBUX SINGH, Chair, Commission for Racial Equality

There are two preconditions for the successful creation of a peaceful, cohesive, prosperous multiracial society. First: the liberation of the talents of all our young people. Second: the ability of all our young people successfully to live and work together. Racism disrupts both.

OFSTED has produced vital evidence showing that race-specific underachievement still blights many pupils from ethnic minority communities (Gillborn and Gipps 1996); and also evidence that schools and local education authorities still remain unclear about how to respond to this (OFSTED 1999). It has done the education service and race relations a great service in bringing forward these two seminal pieces of work.

Despite these two landmarks, the CRE and many others have for a considerable time been concerned that while excellent focused work on raising standards and racial equality was being delivered by OFSTED, there continued to be a failure to integrate these issues into the regular inspections of schools and into the reporting of these inspections. This concern coincided with the publication in 1999 of the Home Secretary's Action Plan for implementing the recomendations of the Stephen Lawrence Inquiry Report (Macpherson, 1999). That Action Plan gave OFSTED a clear lead role in reporting on and helping remove racial disadvantage in education. Failure to integrate race equality into mainstream OFSTED activity would not bode well for the likely success of OFSTED in acquitting its new responsibility.

Because of this concern the CRE commissioned Professor Audrey Osler and Dr Marlene Morrison of the University of Leicester's Centre for Citizenship Studies in Education to conduct research into

OFSTED's inspection processes – and this is the report of their research. The findings give cause for serious concern. The recommendations made in the report indicate how OFSTED can move race equality from its margins into its mainstream and thereby enhance OFSTED's task of raising standards in schools.

The research shows that school inspection reports often fail to report on those aspects of race equality that the OFSTED inspection framework itself requires them to inspect. When they do report on them they do so with little consistency and often with little rigour. Whether or not race equality outcomes are inspected or reported on appears often to depend on the interest and understanding of the particular reporting inspector – the team leader of a group of inspectors in a school. Inspectors themselves seem to feel unprepared and untrained to meet the race equality requirements of their own inspection framework and are keen for training to enhance their skills and understanding. Head-teachers appear to be largely unaware that inspectors will inspect race equality outcomes, and the inspection of these issues, when it occurs, rarely provides them with Key Action points.

This is profoundly disappointing. OFSTED itself, in its 1996 report by Gillborn and Gipps, clearly established the agenda that needs to be addressed. In 1999 OFSTED itself again demonstrated the failure of schools and local education authorities to respond. A consistent systematic effort should have followed, to ensure that progress is driven by inspection.That this appears not to have happened represents a serious failure on the part of OFSTED that needs urgently to be addressed by HMCI.

Government, in responding to the Stephen Lawrence Inquiry Report has decided to introduce new, strengthened race relations legislation. It is confidently expected that new law coming onto the statute book in the autumn of 2000 will place an enforceable statutory duty on public authorities to achieve race equality outcomes. Inspectorates, including OFSTED, are likely to have a key role in inspecting the degree of success that related public authorities have in meeting their new responsibilities. This development will place on OFSTED a new, rigorous requirement to mainstream race equality into its inspection regime. The CRE hopes that the findings and recommendations of this report will help OFSTED prepare for its new enhanced role.

Getting race equality right is not always easy. Even organisations like OFSTED, with a track record of leadership and achievement in the field, can sometimes fall short of what is needed. The CRE brings this report forward as a positive, constructive contribution to helping OFSTED meet its own high standards and as a contribution to eliminating racism from our education system.

I hope that the report can form the basis for a programme of partnership work between the CRE and OFSTED to make school inspection an instrument of change that will serve the whole community.

July 2000

EXECUTIVE SUMMARY
A Report for the Commission for Racial Equality

1. Introduction
Context

The research set out to investigate the extent to which OFSTED school inspection reports apply the sections of the inspection framework relating to race equality, and the quality of such reporting. The research took place between August 1999 and April 2000, during which time OFSTED introduced a new inspection framework in January 2000. This research addresses this new inspection framework and considers its potential to report on race equality. It reports also on processes of inspection under the previous framework, drawing on the experiences and perspectives of HMI, contracted inspectors, headteachers and local education authority advisers.

Thirty inspection reports are analysed of schools in three local education authorities (LEAs), all carried out under the previous framework. The three LEAs selected were a London borough in which a substantial proportion of the school population is from ethnic minority communities; a new unitary authority in the south of England where the proportion of pupils from ethnic minority communities is close to the national average; and a shire county in the Midlands, in which the school population is predominantly white.

Legislation introduced in the late 1980s and 1990s promoted assessment procedures and the publication and interpretation of school-based data designed to make schools more accountable. Increasingly, race equality initiatives also focused on the relative attainment of ethnic minority pupils and on the differential achievement between groups. A new national programme of school inspections was introduced in 1993. The 1996 Schools Inspection Act set out a broad framework for school inspections focusing on quality, standards, the management of financial resources and the spiritual, moral, social and cultural development of pupils. In March 1999 the Government, in its response to the Stephen Lawrence Inquiry Report (Macpherson 1999), gave OFSTED a lead role in monitoring the implementation of strategies designed to prevent and address racism in schools (Home Office, 1999).

Aims and objectives

The research set out to establish:

- The ways in which OFSTED is fulfilling the responsibilities given to it by Government to raise standards by preventing and addressing racism in schools

- The extent to which the OFSTED inspection framework requirements, as they relate to race equality, are reflected in the inspection reports of primary, secondary, and special schools

- The extent to which members of contracted inspection teams are familiar with the implications of the inspection framework for race equality in schools

- The extent to which headteachers understood the resulting assessments of race equality as a feature of inspection and the importance attached to it by inspectors

- The extent to which the reporting of best and worst practice supported or inhibited the reporting of race equality outcomes under the previous framework, and the implications of this for the effectiveness of the current framework and subsequent school-based developments.

Research design and methodology

Evidence was collected from:

- A range of OFSTED documents

- A sample of 60 school inspection reports, from three LEAs, of which 30 were analysed in depth

- Interviews with six OFSTED personnel, including three members of the senior management team

- Interviews with six contracted inspectors

- Interviews with ten headteachers of schools from our sample of 60 schools

- Interviews with three senior LEA officers.

The interviews with OFSTED personnel, inspectors, LEA advisers and headteachers enabled much of the documentary sources on which the research drew to be contextualised and cast light on the processes of inspection as seen from their varied perspectives.

2. The current and previous inspection frameworks

OFSTED's lead role in preventing racism

The Government has given a lead role to OFSTED in the prevention of racism through education. The Government accepted the recommendation of the Stephen Lawrence Inquiry Report that OFSTED inspections include examination of how schools implement strategies to prevent racism in education. Yet it is difficult to see how contracted inspectors will fulfil this duty since it would appear that neither they nor headteachers have been officially informed of it. There is no mention of it on the OFSTED web-site or in *Update*, the regular newsletter issued to inspectors. The Annual Report of Her Majesty's Chief Inspector of Schools 1998-99 made no reference to the Stephen Lawrence Inquiry Report, published earlier that year, or to OFSTED's designated lead role in reporting on race equality provision in schools.

Educational inclusion

The current inspection framework, which came into operation in January 2000 has a number of additional features that could potentially contribute to greater race equality in schools. It adopts the term 'educational inclusion' to cover a range of equality issues, including race equality. Yet this document, and most of the other material issued by OFSTED, fails to discuss racism or its impact on learners of whatever ethnic background.

Silence on racism

The failure of OFSTED to name and discuss racism and 'openly and adequately to recognise and address its existence and causes by policy, example and leadership' (Macpherson, 1999: para. 6.34) places it and its contracted inspectors in a weak position to fulfil the lead role given to it by Government. It is difficult to see how OFSTED and its leadership can contribute to the prevention of racism through the inspection of schools while OFSTED continues to avoid any direct discussion of racism in its standard policy documents and public statements. While OFSTED has published focused research (Gillborn and Gipps, 1996) and conducted thematic inspections on the achievement of ethnic minority pupils (OFSTED 1999), these have not yet informed its work overall.

3. HMI perspectives on race equality and school inspection
Race equality and educational inclusion

Members of HMI lead the researchers to understand that equality will be a key feature of educational inclusion. The notion of 'educational inclusion' is to underpin training for contracted inspectors, although the timetable for this training has yet to be confirmed and it has not been made clear whether it will be mandatory. Evidence from interviews suggests that race equality is not recognised by all at OFSTED as a central feature of educational inclusion. Currently, race equality is seen by members of the OFSTED senior management team not as one key principle underpinning standards in education but as one of a number of 'baubles on the Christmas tree' of school inspection which, although important, may cause the tree to topple over.

Ethnic monitoring

There remains, under the current inspection framework, little guidance on monitoring by ethnicity or on the use to which ethnic data may be put by inspectors. Members of HMI stress how this new framework encourages inspectors to evaluate a school's practices and identify differential achievement. Nevertheless, there appears to be a conflation, in the minds of some HMI, of the requirements to include ethnic composition among the characteristics of a school and the processes of monitoring by ethnicity. It is these processes of ethnic monitoring which would reveal any differentials between groups in attainment, in access to the school's services and provisions, and in the use of disciplinary procedures such as exclusion. However, the failure of schools to collect these data is rarely reported on. There are some uncertainties within OFSTED as to whether regular school inspection is capable of revealing evidence of racial harassment and bullying, which is something that the Government requires OFSTED to monitor.

A common language of race equality

HMI recognises the need for 'a common language' when discussing issues of race equality. Yet some members of HMI, including members of the OFSTED senior management team, themselves lack confidence in using such a language. Race equality has yet to become a central part of the corporate culture and discourse within OFSTED.

4. Inspectors' perspectives

Inspectors were agreed that both the former and the current inspection frameworks permit the inspection of race equality issues in schools. They argued that the degree to which such issues are to be found in reports depends, firstly, on the sensitivity of individual contracted inspectors to such issues and, secondly, on the degree of importance which the reporting inspector as team leader attaches to race equality. Although the former inspection schedule provided a common framework for reporting on race equality and other equalities issues, lack of experience and/or expertise among contracted inspectors meant that, in practice, the benefits of such a common framework were often lost to schools. Having a new inspection framework does not overcome these deficiencies in experience and expertise.

Training needs

Inspectors argued that they needed specific training on race equality issues if they were to be effective in these matters. They were also of the opinion that schools needed training on race equality and, in particular, on the value and importance of ethnic monitoring as part of their efforts to improve the quality of education and overall educational standards.

English as an Additional Language

Inspectors recognised the importance of inspecting EAL provision, but were concerned that it was often designated to someone who lacked the specific skills and expertise to make accurate judgements, based on the evidence, of EAL provision by the school. In particular, concerns were expressed about the quality of reporting in schools where the numbers of pupils needing such provision were small.

Race equality and white schools

It was generally recognised by inspectors that race equality issues in white schools were of considerable importance but they believed that such schools needed further guidance from OFSTED on this aspect of their provision. Inspectors felt that within the time constraints of inspection it was particularly difficult to make judgements about the effectiveness of race equality measures in such schools.

Pupils' spiritual, moral, social and cultural development

This was generally recognised by inspectors as the part of the inspection framework where provision for race equality, and particularly cultural diversity, might be inspected. A number of concerns were raised, however. These related to the extent to which this aspect of the framework might encourage inspectors to view pupils from ethnic minority communities as presenting attitudinal or behavioural problems to schools. Inspectors believed that associating race equality primarily with the spiritual, moral, social and cultural development of pupils distracted from two key issues. The first is the need to ensure high standards for all pupils, regardless of ethnicity, and the second is the need for schools themselves to make structural changes in order to guarantee equality of access to everything the school has to offer.

Racial harassment and bullying

Inspectors recognised that the collection of evidence on racial harassment and bullying was difficult within the constraints of the inspection time-scale and resources.

School management

Inspectors also recognised that the effectiveness of a school's provision in promoting race equality and addressing racism was likely to depend on the leadership of the headteacher.

Failing schools

It was generally believed by contracted inspectors that inadequacies in a school's provision for race equality was unlikely to lead to a judgement that the school was failing or in need of special measures.

Leadership

Inspectors were not convinced that the OFSTED leadership recognised race equality as an essential component of quality in education. They looked to its leadership actively to support them in developing this aspect of educational and social inclusion.

5. School Inspection reports

A pervasive feature of the inspection reports analysed was standardisation of format. Schools provided 'satisfactory', 'sound', 'good', or 'very good' 'value for money'. If they did not reach 'satisfactory' in accordance with most of the judgement criteria, they were judged as needing 'special measures'. Except for one school in the latter category, all schools had 'strengths' which 'outweighed' their 'weaknesses', and both these and the *Key Issues for Action* were expressed qualitatively. In the final report, overall judgements applied a language that rarely prioritised issues of race or addressed attainment by specific ethnic groups. Although differentials in attainment were identified in the text of some reports, the tendency was for such issues to become hidden in stock phrases like 'the need to raise improvement for all' or the need for greater recognition of 'cultural diversity' in a school's curriculum. This was especially the case in the sections of the reports on *Main Findings* and *Key Issues for Action*.

The 'key indicators' provide the main source of statistical data; among the more recent reports analysed this was presented in a comparative form with national averages, similar schools, and all schools. Key Stage, test and examination results provided the main source of comparative data. The reporting of differential attainment by ethnicity was significantly absent from inspection reports.

Also absent from reports was the term 'race equality'. Our findings are supported by an OFSTED-based text search for the term race equality in 10,623 reports between 1997 and 1999, which found the terms racial equality or race equality in only 0.25per cent of the reports. Elements of race equality were implicit in the concept of equal opportunities, mostly in relation to access. Equality of opportunity was embedded in the reports but it did not constitute a prime focus. Racial equality was, in effect, marginal and often wholly absent.

Data on ethnicity was inconsistently applied. Critically, precise numerical data on the ethnic composition of pupil populations were significantly lacking. Where data was used, this was most frequently to define the characteristics of a school and its catchment area, rather than to consider pupils' attainment, achievements or progress. Without precise data, observations that ethnic minority pupils 'hold their own' or that 'some reach very high standards' were relatively meaningless judgements. Consequently it was difficult to establish the extent to which a school, or its curriculum, matched the needs of its pupils.

The needs of pupils with English as an additional language (EAL) were not always addressed coherently. The distinction between pupils with special educational needs and those for whom English is an additional language was not always clear. In the absence of precise evidence from the inspection reports, it is difficult for a reader to establish the extent to which sufficient and appropriate EAL support is being given. It is also difficult to assess the impact of a school's provision on pupils' performance.

6. Headteachers' perspectives

Prior to inspection, headteachers in the research sample did not generally anticipate that equality issues in general, or race equality in particular, were likely to be a feature of inspection. In only one of the schools visited was an issue of race equality identified as a Key Issue for Action. These headteachers reported that in working to promote race equality they would value greater Government leadership.

Inspector training

The headteachers felt that while OFSTED should monitor the strategies used to address and prevent racism in schools, this will only be done sensitively and professionally if contracted inspectors are given appropriate training.

The role of LEAs

For schools to be able to act on any negative assessments they will need follow-up support and advice from external advisers, particularly from their local education authority advisory services.

Ethnic monitoring

Interviews with headteachers indicate that not all recognise the value of ethnic monitoring of pupils' attainments and achievements. Some headteachers do not recognise that monitoring by ethnicity is an important tool which can support the processes of target setting. The current 2000 OFSTED framework does not require them to monitor pupils' attainments by ethnicity, nor are they issued with advice by Government on how this might be done effectively.

Headteacher support and training

A number of the headteachers in our sample acknowledged that they need training and support if they are effectively to challenge inequalities and address and prevent racism through education.

7. Recommendations
To the Department for Education and Employment

- Provide detailed guidance to schools on the purposes and practicalities of monitoring pupils' attainment and achievements by ethnicity, as a key aspect of improving standards in schools

- Require and resource schools to introduce ethnic monitoring within a specified time-scale and to respond to any inequalities in attainment and provision it identifies

- Require and facilitate the ethnic monitoring of teacher employment

- Publicise to schools OFSTED's Government-designated lead responsibility for monitoring strategies to address and prevent racism in schools

- Ensure that LEAs are provided with appropriate resources to follow up and support schools which receive critical assessments of their provision for race equality

- Resource training for headteachers on race equality issues, giving priority to the needs of both the headteachers in schools which are experiencing changes in their ethnic composition (for example, the enrolment of refugees and asylum seekers) and to those who work in predominantly white communities

- Establish an independent, publicly accountable working group to evaluate the 'impact of inspection' processes and reporting on race equality in education.

To OFSTED

- Publicise to contracted inspectors and the wider educational community OFSTED's designated lead responsibility for monitoring strategies to address and prevent racism in schools

- Encourage a corporate culture and discourse of race equality within OFSTED

- Recognise and promote race equality as a central feature of the drive to improve standards in schools

- Require schools to systematically monitor their provision by ethnicity, including pupil attainment and the school's use of sanctions such as exclusion

- Expand OFSTED's definition of educational inclusion in the context of inspection to address how all learners, and particularly learners in predominantly white schools, might be encouraged to challenge racism and promote race equality

- Routinely include a comment on issues of race equality in that part of the school inspection reports sent to parents

- Provide guidance to inspectors and headteachers on indicators of race equality in schools, including indicators in predominantly white schools

- Provide guidance to inspectors and schools on ethnic monitoring as an essential feature of school inspection and school self-evaluation

- Ensure that training for contracted inspectors on educational inclusion is mandatory

- Ensure that race equality is an explicit feature of mandatory training for contracted inspectors

- Enhance inspector training on race equality with regular instructions and guidance, made available on the OFSTED web-site and in regular OFSTED publications such as *Update*

- Ensure that all inspectors required to inspect EAL provision are given appropriate training

- Amend the pre-inspection parents' questionnaire to include an assessment of equalities initiatives in general and provision for race equality in particular

- Where appropriate, invite parents to comment on a school's EAL provision

- Review whether regular school inspections are, in practice, an effective means of monitoring schools' strategies to prevent racial harassment and bullying and, if not, arrange for a special HMI inspection of this provision

- Ensure that race equality issues are given priority in early reviews of the new inspection framework and in reviews of contracted inspectors' reports

- Conduct or commission further research on how OFSTED might most effectively monitor strategies to prevent and address racism in schools

- Require inspectors to identify in their reports successful strategies adopted by schools to promote race equality

- Require inspectors to establish whether those attending the pre-inspection parents' meeting are representative of the school population in terms of ethnicity

- Require inspectors to provide interpretation services wherever this is appropriate to ensure parents' full participation in pre-inspection meetings

To schools

- Develop self-evaluation tools on race equality

- Encourage dialogue between teachers, parents and governors on ways of promoting race equality in the school

- Engage in discussion with OFSTED inspectors about race equality initiatives and the self-evaluation tools the school has developed, viewing inspection as an additional opportunity for professional dialogue

- Use and apply the CRE Standards for Racial Equality in Schools, *Learning for All* (CRE 1999)

References

Commission for Racial Equality (1999) *Learning for All.* CRE

Gillborn, D and Gipps, C (1996) *Recent Research on the Achievements of Ethnic Minority Pupils.* London: OFSTED

Home Office (1999) *Stephen Lawrence Inquiry: Home Secretary's Action Plan.* London: Home Office

Macpherson, W *et.al.* (1999) *The Stephen Lawrence Inquiry: Report of an Inquiry by Sir William Macpherson.* London, Stationery Office

OFSTED (1999) *Raising the Attainment of Minority Ethnic Pupils; school and LEA responses.* London: OFSTED

Chapter 1

INTRODUCTION

This report is the outcome of a research study that was commissioned by the Commission for Racial Equality (CRE) in
August 1999. The CRE's interest is in the extent to which
school inspection reports consistently apply those sections of the
inspection handbooks, the framework (OFSTED 1999a, b and c) that
relate to race equality, and the quality of such applications. During the
course of the research, OFSTED introduced a new framework, *Inspecting Schools* (1999d). Our report thus takes account of the important
changes. Our research is a detailed examination of OFSTED's responsibilities in preventing racism through education, and the potential
of the previous framework (1996-1999) and current (2000) framework
as a means of realising racial equality in schools.

Structure of the Report

The report comprises seven chapters, prefaced by an *Executive Summary* that provides a brief account of the research.

Chapter one is the Introduction. Here, the aims of the research and the
contexts in which it took place are identified and the methods outlined.

In *chapter two*, we examine OFSTED's responsibilities in preventing
racism through education, and we apply a commentary that draws
upon a detailed examination of key OFSTED documents.

The focus for *chapter three* is the perspectives of Her Majesty's
Inspectorate (HMI) on race equality and school inspection. Here, we
draw on interviews with senior OFSTED personnel.

Chapter four provides an analysis of interview data from inspectors
that draws on the depth and breadth of understanding among inspec-

tors under contract to OFSTED who are required to take a lead role in enabling schools to realise race equality.

In *chapter five* we report on a detailed document analysis of thirty reports of schools inspected between 1996-1999, accessed from publicly available web-site information and from data supplied by the Research Department at OFSTED.

Headteachers are the focus of analysis in *chapter six*. The perspectives of ten head teachers in three local education authorities are enhanced by the perspectives of three senior local education authority (LEA) officers from the authorities in which we worked.

A synthesis of our cumulative evidence is the starting point for *chapter seven*, in which the **Conclusions** for the report are given, together with **Recommendations** for the intended audiences for our report namely, DfEE, OFSTED, inspectors under contract to OFSTED, and schools.

The *Appendices* contain an additional range of information about the methodology, for example, interview schedules; illustrative documents; and analytical approaches that informed data collection.

Aims and objectives of the research

The report draws upon evidence from four key focal points of research interest:

First, the study sought to determine the extent to which OFSTED's framework requirements, as they relate to race equality, were reflected in *Section 10* reports of primary, secondary, and special schools, and the consistency and adequacy with which this was achieved. The study also examines how OFSTED is fulfilling the responsibilities given to it by Government to prevent and address racism in schools.

Second, the study also examined the extent to which members of inspection teams, under contract to OFSTED, were familiar with the framework and its implications for inspection, as it relates to race equality.

Third, the study addressed the extent to which inspected schools had understood the resulting assessments of race equality as a feature of

2

schools inspection, and of the importance attached to it by the inspectors.

Fourth, the study considered the extent to which the earlier framework, and particularly its emphasis on the general reporting of 'best' and 'worst' practice, supported or inhibited the reporting of race equality outcomes, and the implications of such evidence for both the current (2000) framework and subsequent school-based developments.

Evidence to demonstrate objectives

Our analysis drew upon four main kinds of evidence.

1. *Documentary-focused evidence to demonstrate:*

- OFSTED's responsibilities in preventing and addressing racism through education and the potential of the OFSTED inspection framework as a means of realising racial equality and racial justice in schools as one important way of raising standards

- the frequency and consistency with which *Section 10* reports reported on race equality and the quality of that reporting

- the frequency of reporting on race equality issues within reports and the inspection categories in which such issues were referred to specifically and generally

- the extent to which ethnic monitoring data was used by inspectors as part of reporting procedures, and whether and how attention was drawn to instances where such data was unavailable

- examples of effective and ineffective practice in the reporting of race equality

2. *Inspector-focused evidence to demonstrate:*

- the depth and breadth of understanding shown by different categories of inspectors about the relevant requirements of the inspec - tion framework

- inspectors' assessments of the extent to which the practice of highlighting the best and worst practice generally impacted upon their coverage of race equality in inspection reports

3

- inspectors' assessments of the extent to which schools understood and felt confident to act upon the reports they were given

- inspectors' assessments of the extent to which they used schools' monitoring data as part of reporting procedures.

3. School-focused evidence to demonstrate:
- the importance in school-based practice of having detailed reports on race equality elements within the school inspection framework

- the extent to which schools understood, and felt confident to act on the basis of the reports they were given in order to improve their practice

- schools' assessment of the extent to which schools were made aware of race equality as a feature of school inspection, and the importance attached to it by inspectors

- headteacher assessments of the extent to which the importance of the relation between inspection and race equality issues permeated beyond the position of headteacher and senior management team to include all staff and members of the governing body.

4. LEA-focused evidence to consider:
- the importance for LEA and school-based practice of having detailed reporting on race equality within the inspection framework.

Context

The starting point to our research has been that, until recently, attempts to challenge racism in schools have been frequently perceived as controversial and have not always received coherent support from central government. The political and educational contexts have been those in which black and ethnic minority pupils rather than educational structures and systems have been assumed to be the real problem (Osler,1997).

In the 1970s and 1980s, local authorities tended to be the agencies who sought to develop policy and practice to promote greater racial justice, ·for example, through pastoral and curriculum initiatives. The Education Reform Act 1988 and subsequent legislation changed the basis of the relationship between schools and LEAs, whilst the introduction and implementation of the National Curriculum effectively ended many individual, often disparate, school-based curricular initiatives designed to promote racial justice. The legislation has also had the effect, especially through its assessment procedures and the publication and interpretation of attainment data, of highlighting issues of accountability for schools. Thus the race equality agenda now increasingly focuses upon the relative achievements of minority groups, and ways to improve their attainment.

As importantly, the cycle of school inspections which began in 1993 has offered a critical instrument for assessing race equality linked to inspection, as a means of raising standards. Inspections are conducted according to a standards framework that embraces: the quality of education provided by the schools; the educational standards achieved; the ways in which financial resources are managed; and the spiritual, moral, social and cultural development of pupils (Schools Inspection Act 1996).

Three years after its inception, OFSTED published a review of the achievement of ethnic minority pupils (Gillborn and Gipps,1996) and was subsequently asked by the Department for Education and Employment (DfEE) to follow up some of the key issues highlighted by that review and by a Home Office Report on problems of racial tension and harassment in schools by the Racial Attacks Group (Home Office, 1996). A dominant theme of the report relates to the mismatch between written school policies and their translation into effective practice. The report also highlights examples of effective practice.

Most recently, as part of the Government's action plan (Home Office, 1999) in response to the recommendations of the Stephen Lawrence Inquiry Report, OFSTED has been given lead responsibility in examining the strategies to prevent and address racism in schools (recommendation 69). In addition, all local authorities are required to be inspected by 2001: the key focus will be upon their role in supporting schools to maintain standards.

As part of the framework for inspection, there are a number of key issues that relate to equality and social justice. Among them, it is clear from the recent Home Office Action Plan (1999) that the Government's intention in relation to race equality is that inspectors are particularly required to gather evidence and report about:

- the extent to which schools have effective measures to promote discipline and good behaviour, and eliminate oppressive behaviour that includes harassment and bullying

- pupils' behaviour, including the incidence of bullying

- the quality of relationships in the school, 'including the degree of racial harmony, where applicable'

- the extent to which statutory requirements are met for all pupils.

The national inspection system includes the concept of a 'failing school'. In order to meet the recommendations of the Stephen Lawrence Inquiry Report, inspectors will need to take specific account of the following issues in deciding whether a school is 'failing to give its pupils an acceptable standard of education' and thus in need of Special Measures. These include:

- regular disruption, breakdown of discipline, or high levels of exclusions

- significant levels of racial harassment and tension

- pupils at physical or emotional risk from other pupils or adults at school.

Certain terms like 'significant' 'regular' and 'breakdown' will require careful explication by inspectors in their contacts with schools and their analyses of school-based evidence. Moreover, even where schools are judged to be acceptable overall, inspectors have been required, since September 1997, to report on schools that have serious weaknesses. The term implies the inclusion of evidence that there may be insufficient or appropriate measures to promote race equality and harmony. The current inspection framework, introduced in January 2000, also includes the concept of an 'underachieving' school. A school might be considered to be underachieving if, for example, pupils from a particular ethnic group were consistently under-performing in relation to their peers.

OFSTED's response to the Stephen Lawrence Inquiry Report recommendations (Home Office, 2000) to put into place training for inspectors strongly suggests a view that there is the need for more training in relation to the effective role of education in realising racial equality, and the contribution of inspection in ensuring that education plays that role consistently.

To summarise, while legislation of the 1980s and 1990s has introduced a largely prescribed curriculum and given schools more autonomy in certain aspects of decision-making, schools are responsible for ensuring that they develop and instigate measures that ensure race equality and racial harmony in the school community. OFSTED's role is to ensure that these and other requirements are met, and the Action Plan completed within forty days of the report provides an appropriate and developmental response that includes an assessment of progress against planned targets.

Research design and methodology

The research design reflects our intention to secure four main kinds of research evidence, as illustrated in an earlier section. This combined a detailed content analysis of inspection reports with a qualitative approach to the collection of primary data using semi-structured interviews as the main research tool. Our intention was for each stage of the research to be mutually informing.

Literature review and document analysis

OFSTED documents

The research process was informed by a literature review that included detailed analyses of key documents from OFSTED. These are listed at the beginning of chapter two.

School inspection reports

Our focus was upon a sample of school reports from three local education authorities, described in the report as LEA1, LEA2, and LEA3. LEA1, a London borough with multiple indices of socio-economic deprivation, was selected because its school population includes a substantial proportion of pupils from ethnic minority backgrounds. LEA2 was selected as an authority in which the proportion of pupils from ethnic minority communities is close to the national average. It is a recently established unitary authority in an expanding town in the South. LEA 3 is a shire county in the Midlands, selected because its school population is predominantly white. In selecting the LEAs, attention was given to geographical location, and to rural/suburban dimensions; the three authorities were considered not untypical of the constituencies they represent.

From an initial selection of 60 maintained school reports (20 from each authority), 30 reports (10 from each authority) were analysed in depth. Within each authority, four reports were of secondary schools, five were of primary schools, and one was of a special school. For the years 1997-1999, selection was by school sector, by year of inspection, and by most recent inspection. Twenty-eight reports were of inspections during 1997-1999, two took place in 1996 because more recent data was unavailable on the web-site. Of the schools selected, one had been judged to require special measures.

In brief, there were five stages to the analysis of school inspection reports.

1. Requests were made to the OFSTED Research Department to provide Pre-Inspection Context and School Indicator (PICSI) data and school profile data on sixty schools. This was received. An additional request was made to scan reports for a number of terms like 'race equality'. For the years 1997-1999, 10,623 inspection reports from the OFSTED data base were scanned.

2. Thirty reports were also scanned by the research team to give an initial indication of the frequency with which terms such as the following were used: 'race' and 'racial equality', 'racism', 'racial harmony', 'ethnic minority', 'ethnic diversity'. This provided an initial indicator of use in reports.

3. Since stage 2 provided limited indicators and context, each of the thirty reports was studied in depth in order to explore the use of the terms, together with other report statements in context.

4. A series of questions were posed (shown as Appendix item 4) and these, in turn, were linked to written evidence from the reports.

Each question was considered as the basis for a framework in which issues of race equality and social justice could be linked to the key concerns of inspection.

5. The fifth stage of the analysis was to examine reports as written accounts that had passed through stages of construction, categorisation and standardisation, and to consider implications for judgements about equality, specifically race equality issues.

Interviews

We conducted interviews in four broad categories, as follows:

a) Interviews took place with senior OFSTED personnel. We interviewed three members of the OFSTED senior management team and three other members of HMI.

b) Interviews took place with six contracted inspectors variously designated as an OFSTED inspection trainer, a registered inspector, team members who had taken on specific responsibilities for coordinating equal opportunities as part of the inspection team, and a lay inspector. We deliberately sought out interviewees from ethnic minority backgrounds. These comprised three of our interviewees – two African Caribbeans and one of Asian descent.

c) School-focused data was collected from ten headteachers of schools from our sample of sixty schools. Care was taken to ensure that interviewees were drawn from a range of schools.

d) Finally, interviews took place with three senior LEA officers located in the authorities from which our schools were selected. Here, the purpose was to obtain contextual data as well as further understanding about the importance of race equality issues in inspection.

The interview schedules for inspectors and headteachers are shown as Appendix items 1 and 2.

These comments conclude our introduction to the report, and the research upon which it is based. In the next chapter, a detailed examination of OFSTED's responsibilities in preventing racism through education provides the key focus for analysis.

Chapter 2

THE OFSTED INSPECTION
FRAMEWORK AND RACE EQUALITY

This chapter examines the responsibilities given by Government to OFSTED to prevent racism through education. It considers the potential of the OFSTED inspection framework as a means of monitoring and enabling race equality initiatives in schools. The research draws on a number of key documents published by OFSTED. These include *The Annual Report of Her Majesty's Chief Inspector of Schools 1998-99; The Framework for the Inspection of Schools* (OFSTED, 1995) in use until the end of 1999; the new framework, *Inspecting Schools* (OFSTED, 1999d), which became effective from January 2000; the handbooks for inspecting primary, secondary and special schools (OFSTED, 1999a; 1999b; 1999c) which also became effective from January 2000; and a briefing paper published by OFSTED (2000b), entitled *Educational Inclusion and School Inspection*.

The context

The new framework, *Inspecting Schools* (OFSTED, 1999d) is introduced at a time when the British government, along with its European partners, is developing policies which emphasise the importance of education as a means of ensuring social inclusion and preventing social exclusion (Social Exclusion Unit, 1998; European Commission, 1997). The Government requires schools to raise standards and achieve greater inclusion. Within this drive to raise standards there is a strong emphasis on target setting. In February 1999 the report of the Stephen Lawrence Inquiry (Macpherson, 1999) identified institutional racism as a major cause of social exclusion in Britain. The publication of the Macpherson Report led senior politicians from a range of political parties to acknowledge institutional racism in British society and the Government pledged itself to a programme to eradicate racism. When presenting the report to the House of Commons, Home Secretary Jack Straw stated:

> The report does not place a responsibility on someone else; it places a responsibility on each of us. We must make racial equality a reality. The vision is clear: we must create a society in which every individual, regardless of colour, creed or race, has the same opportunities and respect as his or her neighbour (Hansard, 24 February 1999: column 393).

Racism is therefore now officially recognised by the Government as a force which operates to restrict the citizenship rights of minorities and which undermines the principles of democracy and inclusion.

Macpherson and OFSTED's lead role in preventing racism

The Macpherson Report made three broad recommendations relating to the role of education in preventing racism. These focused on:

- the amendment of the National Curriculum so that it might prevent racism and reflect the needs of a diverse society

- the prevention of racial harassment and further ethnic monitoring of school exclusion

- the role of OFSTED inspection in these processes.

The Government responded with an action plan, which was reviewed one year on (Home Office, 1999 and 2000). Action points include:

- introducing Citizenship education and reviewing other aspects of the National Curriculum to reflect more adequately the needs of a diverse society

- requiring schools to develop strategies to tackle racial harassment and bullying and have in place effective measures to eliminate oppressive behaviour

- formulating strategies to address the over-representation of certain ethnic minority groups amongst those excluded from school

- providing additional language support and mentoring for ethnic minority children, where required

- reviewing training for teachers and headteachers to ensure that they are able to meet the needs of ethnic minority children

- inspecting schools to ensure that specific strategies are implemented (Home Office, 1999 and 2000: recommendations 66-69).

As Education Minister Jacqui Smith states:

> Education has a crucial role to play in bringing about a fair and just society. It is important that people learn to respect themselves and each other as citizens regardless of their ethnic background (Home Office, Press briefing 033/2000).

Government strategies which, post-Macpherson, aim to challenge racism within society, thus acknowledge the important role education can play in realising race equality. The lead responsibility in monitoring the implementation of race equality initiatives within schools and local education authorities is given to OFSTED (Home Office, 1999 and 2000).

Evidence from HMCI's Report 1998-99 to the Secretary of State for Education

There is, however, no mention of OFSTED's lead role in the prevention of racism through education in the 1998-99 annual report of Her Majesty's Chief Inspector of Schools (OFSTED, 2000a). This is a notable omission, given the recommendations made in the widely publicised Macpherson Report half way through the year in question and confirmed by Government one month later. Nor does HMCI make reference in his commentary to the Ethnic Minority Achievement Grant (EMAG) which is the main funding mechanism for addressing the specific needs of ethnic minority pupils. There is, however, a general reference to 'schools serving disadvantaged communities' where he notes that initiatives such as Education Action Zones and Excellence in Cities 'may have a profound impact' (OFSTED, 2000a: 19). By contrast, the Government's Literacy and Numeracy strategies in primary schools are given a prominent place in HMCI's commentary, even though the latter was not scheduled to come into effect nationally until September 1999, in the following school year.

This annual report of the HMCI is likely to attract the attention of large numbers of decision-makers and opinion formers. It is submitted to the Secretary of State for Education and laid before Parliament, as required by the School Inspection Act 1996. A copy of the 1998-99 report was sent to every maintained school in England. The report is thus potentially very influential and makes a significant contribution to public debate about education. This is recognised by HMCI who, in his covering letter to his 1998-99 report, observed:

> The report begins, as usual, with a commentary on some of the issues of importance. The second section contains the evidence from the year's inspections across the range of matters which fall within my remit.
>
> I hope the report will be of interest to parents, teachers, headteachers, governors and policymakers, as well as contributing to the public debate on standards and quality of education (OFSTED, 2000a).

In a report which emphasises standards in education, the failure to comment on the initial impact of EMAG, a major funding mechanism designed to raise achievement, is curious. Failure to report on the lead responsibility given by Government to OFSTED to prevent racism and ensure inclusion and on the progress OFSTED has made in discharging this responsibility will, for some, raise questions about OFSTED's commitment to this task.

The second section of the report draws on evidence from the year's inspections; here there are references to a number of aspects of school life which relate directly to race equality. These include exclusions, standards and achievement, the teaching of English as an additional language (EAL), the curriculum and pupils' personal development.

Exclusions from school

In the sections on pupils' attitudes and behaviour in both primary and secondary schools, there are references to exclusions. Although, in the section on primary schools, the report notes the disproportionate exclusion of boys, there is no reference, in either the primary or secondary sections, to the disproportionate exclusion of pupils from certain minority communities. Yet this is a long-standing concern of community and parents' organisations. Evidence on this inequality in the use of exclusions was provided to the Stephen Lawrence Inquiry

(Macpherson, 1999). The Department for Education and Employment has been given lead responsibility in this area. In Spring 1999 the Government requested that LEAs develop action plans to address this inequality in the authorities with the highest rate of black exclusions (Home Office, 2000). Also in Spring 1999 the DfEE issued draft guidance on the prevention of exclusions, which addresses the issue of the disproportionate numbers of excluded pupils from particular ethnic groups. This was published as joint statutory guidance from the DfEE, Home Office and Department of Health in July 1999 to come into effect in September of that year (DfEE, 1999). The Government has given OFSTED lead responsibility in monitoring the implementation of this guidance (Home Office, 2000). Although the disproportionate exclusion of certain ethnic groups was overlooked in the 1998-99 report, it might be expected that HMCI's report for 1999-2000 will indicate how schools are fulfilling their new statutory responsibilities, with particular reference to the experiences and needs of ethnic minority pupils.

Racial harassment and bullying

The DfEE guidance also addresses the prevention of racism and the reporting of racist incidents in schools. Again the lead responsibility for monitoring such prevention strategies rests with OFSTED. HMCI notes that secondary schools...

> are increasingly alert to racist behaviour or bullying and generally have appropriate policies. However, the monitoring of the consistency of their implementation is often weak. Though serious incidents involving violence are rare, too many potentially harmful incidents involving name calling or taunting go unchallenged, even when they occur in lessons (OFSTED, 2000a: 42).

Racial harassment in lessons is not just 'potentially harmful'. Such harassment infringes the child's right to security. It may indirectly undermine the right to education itself, if it causes a pupil to fear attending school. This would affect the pupil's learning and achievement. Such behaviour, if unchecked, is harmful not only to the victim but also to the perpetrator. Qualitative research studies have shown that children tend to take such behaviour seriously and are likely to be much more aware of it than the adults who are responsible for their welfare (Troyna and Hatcher, 1992; Osler, 2000a). HMCI observes that most inner city schools have policies 'on education for diversity'. It is disappointing that the report does not take the opportunity to recommend that all schools adopt such policies and practices.

HMCI helpfully acknowledges the importance of 'agreed procedures for dealing with racist behaviour' in the section which addresses primary schools (OFSTED, 2000a: 31). He might usefully bring this to the attention of secondary schools, particularly as it is now a statutory requirement (DfEE, 1999).

Standards and achievement

The HMCI report notes that a number of ethnic minority groups 'underachieve' in primary school. No explanation for this is offered but HMCI observes that 'The use of ethnic monitoring as part of the school strategy for raising attainment has barely begun' (OFSTED, 2000a: 28). The achievement of pupils from particular ethnic minority groups is also noted as 'a matter for concern' in secondary schools (ibid: 37), but in a report where there is a strong overall focus on the need to improve standards we are given no indication of why schools are failing these pupils, nor are examples of good practice in raising the achievement of these groups provided. The report observes that among inner city schools the more effective schools tend to have a higher proportion of pupils from ethnic minority backgrounds than less effective schools, but with no contextual information offered about these schools it is difficult to draw any lessons from this.

English as an additional language

The report notes the need for more systematic tracking of the progress of pupils with EAL in primary schools. It acknowledges the value of the specialist contribution of EAL staff in primary schools in the planning of the Literacy Hour, notably in providing advice on resources, text selection and in training. There is minimal information on EAL teaching in secondary schools, with a passing observation of the value of subject teachers' explicit teaching of specialist terminology, particularly to pupils with EAL. There are no references to the teaching of EAL in the section on sixth forms nor any mention of the needs of ethnic minority pupils.

The curriculum

In the section which addresses secondary schools we are informed by HMCI that 'Most schools provide a broad, balanced and relevant curriculum, *with equality of access and opportunity for all pupils*' (our emphasis). It is difficult to know how this assertion can be supported in the absence of ethnic monitoring procedures or data which might provide information on various ethnic groups' achievements in the different curriculum subjects. The Macpherson Report recommended that 'consideration be given to the amendment of the National Curriculum aimed at valuing cultural diversity and preventing racism, in order to better reflect the needs of a diverse society'. This would seem to imply that we cannot afford to be complacent in assuming that most schools do, in fact, already have such a curriculum in place, or that more cannot be done in this area. There is only one reference to race equality issues in the National Curriculum subject reporting section of the HMCI report, where we are informed that some schools 'do not give sufficient emphasis to non-European history' (OFSTED, 2000a: 41).

Pupils' personal development

HMCI notes that provision for cultural development is good in half the primary schools and just over half of the secondary schools inspected. However, the report identifies a key challenge for schools who need

> to establish an appropriate balance between ensuring pupils understand the cultural traditions of the United Kingdom and preparing them for life in multicultural Britain ...

Where the provision by schools is inadequate:

> The main weakness identified by inspectors is the limited emphasis given to non-Western cultures (OFSTED, 2000a: 32).

The first of these statements implies a tension between the cultural traditions of the United Kingdom and the notion of multiculturalism. It clearly hides a more complex reality. Preparation for life in a multicultural Britain requires much more than an understanding of the cultures of visible minorities. A minimal requirement is a vision of multiculturalism which is inclusive of majority communities and their traditions, as well as those of minorities (Osler, 1999 and 2000b). As we know from the Burnage Report (Macdonald, *et al.*,1989), reductionist and moralistic multicultural and anti-racist approaches in schools are likely to be counter-productive, since they exclude white communities and identities. This seems to be acknowledged by HMCI who writes of the 'outstanding' cultural provision in some schools which 'includes dance, drama, music and poetry from a range of cultural perspectives, often linked to work undertaken in other subjects' (OFSTED, 2000a: 32). We argue that such provision not only needs to be linked to other subjects but also to pupils' own identities and experiences. Preparation for life in multicultural Britain requires that all young people, of whatever ethnicity, have opportunities within their schooling to explore their identities. Education is a process by which individuals expand their range of identities (Osler and Starkey, 1996).

Leadership and management

We understand race equality to be a school management issue. However, there is no reference to equality, diversity or the needs of minorities in the section of HMCI's report on the management and efficiency of either primary or secondary schools. Nor is there any reference to the specific needs of minority groups in the sections which address partnerships with parents and the community.

Special schools

There is no reference to ethnic minority pupils or the particular needs of pupils with EAL in the section of HMCI's report which addresses special schools. No race equality issues are addressed in this section.

Schools with serious weaknesses or requiring special measures

In the section of HMCI annual report for 1998-99 which addresses schools requiring special measures and those with serious weaknesses, mention is made of a number of problems. These include weak leadership and management; shortcomings in the quality of teaching (including low standards, inadequacies in teachers' subject knowledge, and low expectations of pupils); deteriorating pupil behaviour; and poor progress in improving the curriculum. While a number of these relate to aspects of the inspection framework which address race equality

18

issues (see our Table 2.1) the section on schools requiring special measures or with serious weaknesses makes no reference to issues which can be directly identified as racial disadvantage. For example, there are no references to variations in achievement between different ethnic groups within a school; inadequate responses to racial harassment; failure to meet the needs of pupils with English as an additional language; or inequality of access to the curriculum.

General observations

Since the second part of the annual report draws on OFSTED Section 10 school inspection reports, the omission of certain race equality issues from this report may simply reflect that these issues were not highlighted in the *Main Findings* or *Key Issues for Action* sections of the inspection reports on which it draws. These are the sections made available to parents and the ones which also tend to attract the attention of the local and national media. Nevertheless, the low profile of race equality issues in the commentary of HMCI in a year when OFSTED was given a lead role in the Government's strategic plans to eradicate racism is disturbing.

Special schools educate some of the most vulnerable children and young people in our society, many of whom may be at risk of long-term social exclusion. It is therefore critically important that questions of race equality be addressed in these schools and that issues that relate to the particular needs of pupils from minority communities at such schools should not be overlooked.

We are not aware of any briefing to schools, inspection contractors or registered inspectors which highlights OFSTED's lead role in examining strategies to eradicate racism through education. Indeed, we are led to believe that the only public document issued by OFSTED to date that mentions Macpherson is *Educational Inclusion and School Inspection.*[1] This briefing, issued eleven months after the Macpherson report was published, makes no mention of the lead role given by the Government to OFSTED, to monitor strategies to prevent racism within education. It merely refers to the fostering of better personal, community and race relations in schools. The only reference made in the briefing is as follows:

the McPherson (sic) Report which included among its recommendations (67-69) several related to schools and school inspection in valuing
cultural diversity, and reporting on and preventing racism (OFSTED,
2000b: 3, footnote 6).

OFSTED's formal response to Macpherson

The Government's review of progress in the year following the publication of the Stephen Lawrence Inquiry report identifies four key
actions by OFSTED:

1   The revised framework for school inspection 'builds in a much
    stronger focus on inspecting the ways in which schools take
    account of and value pupils' cultural diversity and how they com-
    bat racism'. Inspectors will 'evaluate and report on how effec-
    tively the school makes provision for pupils from minority ethnic
    backgrounds and the standards they achieve'. Schools will be
    required to include 'a breakdown of exclusions for the past year by
    ethnic groups'.

2   'Training material for OFSTED inspectors is being revised and
    will include an emphasis on Educational Inclusion. In addition a
    specific course is being developed entitled 'Educational Inclusion
    and School Inspection' which is expected to be mandatory for all
    inspectors. Training for HMI as part of their continuing profes-
    sional development also incorporates these issues as they relate to
    their work within specific divisions within OFSTED' (Home
    Office 2000: recommendation 69).

3   There will be a summary report in Spring 2000 on special inspec-
    tions of high truancy and excluding schools.

4   OFSTED will monitor the implementation of the anti-bullying
    guidance as part of their programme of regular school inspections
    (Home Office 2000: recommendation 68).

The revised school inspection framework and its capacity to contribute
to race equality issues in schools is discussed later in this chapter,
under the heading 'The OFSTED School Framework and Race
Equality'. At the time of writing OFSTED has yet to publish its training materials on 'educational inclusion', although the briefing paper

on which this is based is discussed in the following section. The Spring 2000 issue of *Update*, an OFSTED publication aimed at Section 10 inspectors and contractors, reports, under the heading 'Educational Inclusion' that:

> OFSTED have identified this subject as one of the highest priority training areas. We are developing a training course for all inspectors, and participation is likely to be mandatory. The course is likely to take the form of a distance learning module, although there may be some pre-course or follow-up work to do too. Training is likely to be available by September 2000 (OFSTED, 2000c).

Nor has the summary report on special inspections of high truancy and excluding schools been published at the time of writing. OFSTED's capacity to monitor the implementation of the anti-bullying guidance as part of its programme of regular school inspections is open to question, and is in fact doubted by one of the HMIs we interviewed for this research (see chapter three, on HMI perspectives). If the anti-bullying guidance cannot be monitored through regular school inspections, then it would seem appropriate that this also be made the subject of a special inspection by HMI.

Educational inclusion and race equality

Educational inclusion

Here we wish to consider the concept of 'educational inclusion' as identified by OFSTED in the revised inspection framework (OFSTED, 1999d) and developed in the briefing paper *Educational Inclusion and School Inspection* (OFSTED, 2000b). In particular we consider whether it adequately addresses race equality in education. OFSTED states that educational inclusion covers:

- equal opportunities (for all pupils regardless of age, gender, ethnicity, attainment, background)

- the education of pupils having English as an additional language

- the education of pupils with special educational needs – including those pupils with challenging and disruptive behaviour

- pupils who are gifted or talented (OFSTED, 2000b).

There are a number of advantages in bringing together the groups of pupils referred to above and discussing their educational needs as a whole. Not least of these is the fact that certain individuals may find themselves in more than one of the above categories. Nevertheless, there is the danger that the specific issue of race equality may be lost among a host of other concerns. It may be argued, for example, that particular ethnic minority groups may have specific group as well as individual needs which require institutional responses and structural change within the school. Thus a school may need to review its dress code in the light of pupils' cultural or religious requirements, so as not to indirectly discriminate against a particular group. Whereas, for a pupil who has a specific learning difficulty or talent, it may be more appropriate for a school to respond on an individual basis.

Inclusion and racial equality in predominantly white schools

In focusing largely on individuals or groups of pupils who are vulnerable to educational exclusion, the briefing paper *Educational Inclusion and School Inspection* (OFSTED, 2000b) largely overlooks issues of race equality in schools whose pupil make-up is predominantly or exclusively white. It is critical that pupils in such schools are also prepared for life in a multicultural society, and indeed are also prepared to work within multicultural settings. Without such elements it is difficult to see how education can effectively contribute to the prevention of racism in society. OFSTED's concept of educational inclusion, as it applies to inspection, is seriously flawed by this oversight. As a consequence, some of these schools may conclude that the prevention of racism and the promotion of race equality are responsibilities that can be ignored with impunity.

Ethnic monitoring

The OFSTED briefing paper on educational inclusion and school inspection advises that in evaluating educational inclusion, inspectors need to be adequately informed about the various groups in a school. If preliminary analysis suggests that there are 'significant differences' among pupils in achievement, access to the curriculum, and other provision, inspectors need to be aware of these differences. It notes that

> The quality of data available from the school varies depending on the emphasis the school places on monitoring the relative attainment of different groups (OFSTED, 2000b: 2).

The quality of data available to inspectors, and the school management's awareness of the importance of monitoring achievement by ethnicity, would seem to be a critical factor in ensuring the inclusion of minorities. It is unfortunate that this key document does not identify as a serious weakness any school's failure to collect data or to monitor by ethnicity.

Institutional racism in education

It is interesting to note that the OFSTED briefing on educational inclusion generally avoids use of the word 'racism' or the term 'race equality'. The one exception is when it quotes from the inspection framework, where in relation to pupils' attitudes, values and personal development, inspectors are asked to consider the extent to which 'pupils work in an atmosphere free from oppressive behaviour, such as bullying, sexism and racism' (OFSTED, 2000b: 6). Although Government has given OFSTED a lead role in preventing racism in education, there is no attempt to define racism within this document, nor is there any discussion of the concept of institutional racism, as it might apply to schools. The closest the document comes to considering this issue is in its discussion of school effectiveness. It states:

> (Inspectors) will need also to consider whether *the school's practice disproportionately disadvantages some individuals or groups of pupils.* This might be reflected in the *attitudes and strategies of some teachers, conscious or not,* or, for example, the way in which behaviour and exclusions are handled (OFSTED, 2000b: 5, our emphasis).

The Stephen Lawrence Inquiry defined institutional racism as:

> The collective failure of an organisation to provide an appropriate and professional service to people because of their colour, culture, or ethnic origin. It can be detected in processes, attitudes and behaviour which amount to discrimination through unwitting prejudice, ignorance, thoughtlessness and racist stereotyping which disadvantage minority ethnic people. It persists because of the failure of the organisation openly and adequately to recognise and address its existence and causes

by policy, example and leadership. Without recognition and action to eliminate such racism, it can prevail as part of the ethos or culture of the organisation. It is a corrosive disease (Macpherson, 1999: para. 6.34).

The 'attitudes and strategies of some teachers, conscious or not', which reinforce any 'practice which disproportionately disadvantages some individuals or groups of pupils' from ethnic minority backgrounds in a school lead to, and cumulatively amount to, institutional racism as defined in the report of the Stephen Lawrence Inquiry.

The Home Secretary, when he presented the Stephen Lawrence Inquiry Report to the House of Commons, acknowledged that institutional racism is a feature of all aspects of society:

> Any long-established, white dominated organisation is liable to have procedures, practices and a culture which tend to exclude or disadvantage non-white people. The police service in this respect is little different from other parts of the criminal justice system, or from government departments ... and many other institutions' (Hansard, 24 February 1999).

If we accept this to be the case then it is critical that schools are encouraged to review their policies and practices to ensure that ethnic minority pupils are not disadvantaged. Ethnic monitoring to identify any differentials in achievement is a first step. This needs to be followed by specific actions to address any such differentials. These actions are essential but not sufficient.

A publication entitled *Inclusive Schools, Inclusive Society: race and identity on the agenda* provides schools with a useful working definition of racism in education, exploring the ways in which it can become institutionalised:

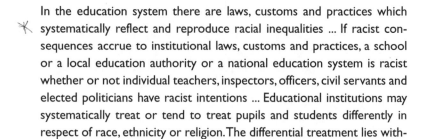

> In the education system there are laws, customs and practices which systematically reflect and reproduce racial inequalities ... If racist consequences accrue to institutional laws, customs and practices, a school or a local education authority or a national education system is racist whether or not individual teachers, inspectors, officers, civil servants and elected politicians have racist intentions ... Educational institutions may systematically treat or tend to treat pupils and students differently in respect of race, ethnicity or religion. The differential treatment lies with-

> in an institution's ethos and organisation rather than in the attitudes, beliefs and intentions of individual members of staff. The production of differential treatment is 'institutionalised' in the way the institution operates (Richardson and Wood, 1999: 33).

Practices to promote educational inclusion need to acknowledge that pupils and their families from minority communities often experience exclusion outside school, as a result of racism in society. Schools therefore need to develop policies and practices which are explicitly anti-racist. An inclusive school must necessarily be anti-racist. It will not only value cultural diversity but also recognise that it needs to challenge discriminatory processes, attitudes and behaviours which work to exclude. There are implications here for the support of teachers. As the Bishop of Stepney, Dr John Sentamu, argues:

> Since the OFSTED framework requires its inspectors to report on the provision in schools for their pupils on moral, spiritual, social and cultural education, no school needs any official justification for developing multi-cultural and racism awareness training programmes. In-service training should be specifically targeted according to the stage of development reached by learners and should not be offered as part of a general awareness-raising strategy (Sentamu, 2000: 52).

Yet OFSTED is silent on the matter of anti-racism. An explicit and unambiguous commitment to anti-racism by OFSTED and its leadership would thus demonstrate that it does, in fact, value cultural diversity in British society. It would set a climate in which schools would be encouraged to make a similar commitment, not as a gesture of 'political correctness' but in recognition that race equality is a principle underpinning inclusivity. As Home Office Minister Mike O'Brien has expressed it:

> Anti-racism is not about helping black and Asian people; it is about our future – white and black. We all live in a multicultural society and we all have a choice: either we make a success of multicultural Britain or we do not. If we fail to address those issues, our children – white and black – will pay the price of that failure. That is why all of us, white and black, have a vested interest in the (Race Relations Amendment) Bill and in anti-racism. We must make Britain a success as a multicultural society (Hansard, 9 March 2000: column 1281).

The Race Relations Amendment Bill will, when passed, place a positive duty on all public bodies to promote race equality.

It is perhaps unfortunate that the OFSTED briefing on *Educational Inclusion and School Inspection* (OFSTED, 2000b) fails to cross-reference the valuable report *Raising the Attainment of Minority Ethnic Pupils: school and LEA responses* (OFSTED, 1999g) which is far more comprehensive than its title might imply. This OFSTED document does recognise the exclusion and discrimination children from minority communities are likely to encounter outside school. As well as discussing initiatives to raise attainment levels in relation to teaching and curriculum, this report also provides examples of good practice in relation to such issues as pastoral care, mentoring, links with ethnic minority parents and communities, racial tensions in the community and racial harassment in schools. Headteachers working in predominantly white communities will also find useful advice and guidance in the report. The report also covers LEA strategies to ensure the inclusion of parents from minority communities, and includes sections on staff recruitment and school exclusions.

It might also be helpful if the OFSTED briefing on *Educational Inclusion and Inspection* were to make reference to the section of the National Curriculum entitled *Inclusion: providing effective learning opportunities for all pupils* (QCA, 1999). This document addresses the need for setting suitable learning challenges, responding to pupils' diverse needs and overcoming potential barriers to learning. It points out, for example, that effective learning environments are those in which all forms of bullying and harassment, including racial harassment, are challenged and pupils are enabled to participate safely, in clothing appropriate to their religious beliefs. It identifies two broad groups of pupils for whom teachers may have to overcome potential barriers to learning: those with special educational needs and those for whom English is an additional language.

It would be helpful if OFSTED were to acknowledge institutional racism in the education service. This, we would argue, is a necessary step if OFSTED is to fulfil the lead role entrusted to it by Government and gather information and report on schools' efforts to prevent racism. In its guidance on educational inclusion, OFSTED also needs to identify and name those processes, attitudes and behaviours which contribute to institutional racism and exclude ethnic minority pupils. Only then can it be confident that inspectors will be able to use the inspection framework evaluation schedule to assess whether processes, attitudes and behaviours which they observe are reinforcing racism and perpetuating racial disadvantage or preventing racism and enabling the inclusion and achievement of ethnic minority pupils.

The OFSTED inspection framework and race equality

Our figure 2.1 summarises those aspects of two OFSTED inspection frameworks that are particularly relevant to promoting race equality. The first of these (OFSTED, 1995) was in operation at the time we commenced this research. The second (OFSTED, 1999d) came in to operation in January 2000. Figure 2.1 draws on an earlier analysis of the 1996-99 inspection framework (Osler, 1997) to summarise those features which support race equality. These are presented in the left-hand column. The right-hand column illustrates those additional features of the current framework which may be used to promote race equality. This earlier analysis concluded that:

> Although inspection may only confirm what the senior management of a school already know concerning strengths and weaknesses, references to equality within the Ofsted guidance may usefully be exploited by those committed to challenging racism.

> ...Interestingly, the Ofsted guidance on equal opportunities is placed within the section on leadership and management, so acknowledging such issues as a responsibility of heads and governors and as a whole school concern (Osler, 1997: 31 and 38).

By studying Figure 2.1 it is possible to identify developments from the previous framework and to identify the types of judgement inspectors are asked to make which may enable them to assess the actions taken by a school which may contribute to racial equality.

There are eight key questions within the inspectors' evaluation schedule of the 2000 framework:

1   What sort of school is it?

2   How high are standards?

3   How well are pupils or students taught?

4   How good are the curricular and other opportunities offered to pupils or students?

5   How well does the school care for its pupils or students?

6   How well does the school work in partnership with parents?

7   How well is the school led and managed?

8   What should the school do to improve further? (OFSTED, 1999d)

By considering each of the first seven of these questions within the evaluation framework it is possible to examine the strengths and weaknesses of the 2000 framework in supporting race equality in schools. The commentary below on each of the questions should be read with reference to Figure 2.1.

What sort of school is it?

Inspectors are now provided with greater guidance on how they should describe the school in terms of ethnic composition. They are required to note the number and proportion of ethnic groups, including refugees and asylum seekers, Travellers and pupils for whom English is an additional language, noting within this last group the numbers of pupils who are at early stages of learning English.

How high are standards?

Within the revised framework there is a sharper focus on the importance of ethnic monitoring, as part of a wider process of collecting data about specific groups of pupils. There is also a greater emphasis on inspectors establishing what schools have actually done, for example, when they have found evidence of differential achievement between ethnic groups. There are, however, some issues relating to the evidence base. The handbooks for inspecting primary, secondary and special schools all state:

> Schools should be judged primarily by their achievements, and on the effectiveness of their teaching, leadership and management in contributing to pupils' progress. Where a school is very effective, there is little need to trawl through all its procedural documents (OFSTED, 1999a: 137; 1999b: 126; and 1999c: 129).

Table 2.1 The OFSTED Inspection Framework and Racial Equality: summary of additional features of 2000 Framework compared with that of 1996-1999

Former Inspection Framework 1996 – 1999	Current Inspection Framework 2000
3.1 Characteristics of the school • Include a description of school composition in terms of pupils' attainment on entry, gender, ethnicity and background.	1. WHAT SORT OF SCHOOL IS IT? • Note the level of pupil mobility. • Include information on social advantage or deprivation. • Note number and proportion of ethnic groups including refugees and asylum seekers, Travellers, pupils with EAL and number of pupils who are at early stages of learning English.
4.1 Attainment and progress • Report on what pupils achieve by 5 years in nursery or reception classes, by the end of each key stage, and by 19 years with reference to attainment. • Highlight any significant variations in attainment among pupils of different gender, ethnicity or background. • Report whether attainment and progress of minority groups is comparable with others.	2. HOW HIGH ARE STANDARDS? *2.1 The school's results and achievements* Consider the extent to which: • the school sets challenging targets and is on course to meet or exceed them • pupils having EAL are making good progress • standards are consistently high across subjects (highlight any variations of achievement by different groups in different subjects • results in the school are high compared with similar schools (or show significant added value in relation to pupils' earlier results).
4.2 Attitudes, behaviour and personal development • Evaluate and report on pupils' response to the teaching and other provision made by the school, highlighting strengths and weaknesses, as shown by the quality of relationships in the school including the degree of racial harmony. • Assess how pupils, including those of different ethnic groups, relate to one another. • Report any inappropriate behaviour including harassment and bullying, towards particular groups of pupils. • Note the level of respect between pupils and teachers and other adults in school, and whether pupils are encouraged to articulate their own views and beliefs. • Are pupils interested in views and ideas different from their own? Do they recognise and understand a diversity of beliefs, attitudes, and social and cultural traditions?	*2.2 Pupils' attitudes, values and personal development* Inspectors must evaluate and report on: • behaviour, including the incidence of exclusions • attendance (including whether some groups are over-represented in relation to exclusions or attendance) Consider the extent to which pupils • show an interest in school life and are involved in the range of activities the school provides • form constructive relationships with one another and with teachers and other adults • work in an atmosphere free from oppressive behaviour such as bullying, sexism, and racism • respect other people's differences, particularly their feelings, values and beliefs • Where there are differences in attitudes to school from different groups, find out why. Is the school aware of them and what attitude is it taking? • Does the school value the cultural traditions, aspirations and values pupils bring from their homes and communities?

29

- Evaluate the extent to which pupils are encouraged to work in mixed ethnic and gender groups.
- Determine whether action by the school has been effective in combating barriers to pupils' full access to, and participation in, the educational opportunities offered.

5.1 Teaching

- Highlight the extent to which teaching meets the needs of all pupils.
- Focus on any pupils for whom English is an additional language.

3. HOW WELL ARE PUPILS TAUGHT?

- Pay particular attention to the needs of specific groups of pupils, including those who have EAL.

Consider the extent to which teachers

- challenge and inspire pupils, expecting the most of them
- use methods which enable all pupils to learn effectively
- use resources which reflect sensitivity to different groups, cultures and backgrounds so as not to demotivate them through inappropriate images or stereotypes.

5.2 Curriculum assessment

- Evaluate and report on the planning and content of the curriculum and its contribution to the educational standards achieved by all pupils.
- Evaluate how curriculum planning and implementation takes account of age, capacity, gender, ethnicity, background, competence in English as an additional language and special educational need.
- Evaluate procedures for assessing pupils' attainment.
- Does the curriculum provide equality of access and opportunity for pupils to learn and to make progress?
- Consider the impact of the organisation of pupils into class and teaching groups on equality of access and opportunity.
- Judge whether careers guidance is objective and free from gender and other stereotyping.

4. HOW GOOD ARE THE CURRICULAR AND OTHER OPPORTUNITIES OFFERED TO PUPILS?

Consider the extent to which the school

- provides a broad range of worthwhile opportunities which meet the interests, aptitudes and particular needs of pupils, including those having SEN
- provides enrichment through its extra-curricular provision, including support for learning outside the school day
- is socially inclusive by assuring equality of access for all pupils
- provides, for secondary aged pupils, effective careers education and guidance, work experience and vocational education
- has links with the community which contribute to pupils' learning
- Does the curriculum ethos affirm and actively respect ethnic, cultural and religious diversity within a socially inclusive school?
- Do any features of curriculum planning advantage or disadvantage different groups of pupils?
- Is there any inequality of access to the curriculum, courses and extra curricular activities?
- Does the school monitor different groups' involvement across the range of activities provided?

5.3 *Pupils' spiritual, moral and social development.*
- Evaluate and report on the strengths and weaknesses of the school's provision for the spiritual, moral, social and cultural development, through the curriculum and life of the school, the example set for pupils by adults in the school.
- Evaluate the quality of collective worship.
- Does the school provide pupils with knowledge and understanding of values and beliefs and enable them to reflect on their experiences to promote spiritual awareness and self-knowledge?
- Does the school teach principles which distinguish right from wrong?
- Does the school encourage pupils to relate positively to each other?
- Are pupils encouraged to take responsibility, participate fully in the school community and develop an understanding of citizenship?
- Are pupils taught to appreciate their own cultural traditions and the diversity and richness of other cultures?

Comment on the extent to which the school cultivates pupils' personal – including spiritual, moral, social and cultural – development
- Does the curriculum promote respect, tolerance and good behaviour?

5.4 *Support, guidance and pupils' welfare*
- Evaluate and report on the school's provision for pupils' educational and personal support and guidance of pupils and its contribution to educational standards.
- Does the school have effective measures to eliminate oppressive behaviour including all forms of harassment and bullying?
- Does the school recognise and record incidents of harassment and bullying that occur, and what steps are taken to prevent repetition?

5. HOW WELL DOES THE SCHOOL CARE FOR ITS PUPILS?
- How effectively does the school monitor pupils' academic performance and personal development?
- Does the school report, monitor and respond effectively to incidents of sexual and racial harassment, bullying and hostile behaviour?
- Explore the reasons for any differences in patterns of behaviour and attendance between groups and assess whether the school's explanations are translated into effective action.
- How is assessment and monitoring used to inform planning for the support needs of EAL learners? Are any additional assessments integrated into the school's normal assessment procedures?
- What is the impact of the school's behavioural policy in promoting respect and tolerance towards others and their beliefs, cultures and ethnic backgrounds?

5.5 Partnership with parents and the community
- Evaluate and report on the effectiveness of the school's partnership with parents.
- Establish whether the school does all it can to gain the involvement of all parents.

6. HOW WELL DOES THE SCHOOL WORK IN PARTNERSHIP WITH PARENTS?
Consider the extent to which
- parents are satisfied with what the school provides and achieves
- parents are provided with good quality information about the school, and particularly about pupils' progress
- links with parents contribute to pupils' learning at home and at school.
- Does the school have the confidence of all parents and the communities it serves? If not, why not?
- Does the school involve parents and carers fully as partners in providing for the needs of their children? If so, how is this achieved? If not, why not?
- What arrangements are made for parents whose first language is not English?
- How well does the school consult parents about its curriculum?

6.1 Leadership and management
- Evaluate and report on how well the governors, headteacher and staff with management responsibilities contribute to the quality of education and standards achieved by all pupils.
- To what extent is there a positive ethos, which reflects the school's commitment to high achievement, an effective learning environment, good relationships and equality of opportunity for all pupils?
- How does the leadership of the school contribute to attitudes, relationships and the provision of equal opportunities?

7. HOW WELL IS THE SCHOOL LED AND MANAGED?
Consider the extent to which
- leadership ensures clear direction for the work and development of the school, and promotes high standards for all
- the school has explicit aims and values, including a commitment to good relationships and equality of opportunity for all, which are reflected in all its work
- the school identifies appropriate priorities and targets, takes the necessary action, and reviews progress towards them
- there is a shared commitment to improvement and the capacity to succeed
- Does the governing body fulfil its statutory responsibilities with regard to equal opportunities legislation?

6.2 Staffing, accommodation and learning resources
- Evaluate and report on the adequacy of staffing, accommodation and learning resources.
- Establish whether teaching and support staff who work with pupils for whom English is an additional language, are experienced and qualified for such work.
- Assess the effectiveness of the staff development and in-service training programme in motivating staff and in meeting individual and corporate needs.

6.3 Efficiency
- Evaluate and report on efficiency and effectiveness with which the resources are managed.
- Pay particular attention to the deployment of additional teaching and support staff for pupils for whom English is an additional language, including any staff financed through special grants.

Consider the extent to which
- learning resources are adequate for the school's curriculum and matched to the range of pupils and their needs.

- Focus on the school's commitment (and action in support of) improvement for all.
- To what extent are educational priorities supported through careful financial management?

Yet, in order to establish whether there is differential achievement between groups of pupils or inequalities in access to the curriculum, the management of the behaviour policy or other provision, inspectors are likely to be heavily dependent on school data or on data collected as part of the pre-inspection process. For example, on the pre-inspection Form S2 schools are required to give the number of fixed-period and permanent exclusions during the school year prior to the inspection, indicating the number of instances of exclusion for boys and girls by ethnic group. Thus this form does not allow the OFSTED inspection team to assess whether a school is conducting systematic ethnic monitoring of exclusions, merely to see that this data is recorded for the past twelve months. Data on the pupils' ethnicity may be recorded, possibly retrospectively, without the school being required to look for patterns or trends. Moreover, inspectors are unlikely to be in a position to identify trends from this data. Form S2 also requires detailed information on standards of attainment, which includes data on the various curriculum subjects. Schools are not, however, required to provide a breakdown of attainment by ethnicity.

An important requirement of the new inspection framework is that inspectors are expected, as part of their assessment of standards, to consider the extent to which pupils work in an atmosphere free from oppressive behaviour such as bullying, sexism and racism. Another useful requirement is that they are asked to judge whether the school values the cultural traditions, aspirations and values which pupils bring from their homes and communities.

How well are pupils taught?

Inspectors are required to consider the extent to which teachers use resources which reflect sensitivity to different groups, so as not to de-motivate them through inappropriate images or stereotypes. Schools are not, however, required or expected to recruit teachers who reflect the diversity of the student body or local community. Schools are expected to be able to provide a detailed breakdown of their pupil composition by ethnicity, but there is no requirement for ethnic monitoring of teaching or non-teaching staff. Although an ethnic 'match' is not necessary in order for pupils to find appropriate role models, schools are more likely to be in the position to meet pupils' needs if there is ethnic and lingustic diversity among the teaching staff. For example, pupils in the early stages of learning English might directly benefit from teachers who speak their home languages.

How good are the curricular and other opportunities offered to pupils?

Figure 2.1 lists a whole new list of requirements against which inspectors are asked to assess the curricular and other opportunities offered to pupils, including the degree to which the school is able to assure equality of access to all. This is an area of the framework which has been considerably strengthened in terms of equal opportunities issues in general.

How well does the school care for its pupils?

This section of the evaluation schedule has also been tightened up. Inspectors are asked to assess how effectively the school monitors pupils' academic performance and personal development, but it is possible to answer this question on an individual basis without checking on whether different ethnic groups experience the curriculum differently. The questions on reporting, monitoring and responding to sexual and racial harassment have been strengthened. Inspectors who can assess schools' actions against the new statutory guidance (DfEE, 1999) will be enabling greater race equality.

Form S3, which is the self-audit headteachers are required to complete before inspection, is divided into two sections: the first is 'statutory requirements', the second 'other areas of school self-audit'. In the section *How well does the school care for its pupils?* listed under statutory requirements, there is no reference to the new statutory guidance on sexual and racial harassment or to other equal opportunities measures. The self-audit questions addressing equality fall into the second category of the form, under 'other areas for school self audit', as if equality of provision for all pupils was not a statutory requirement. This is despite the fact that schools already have legal obligations to ensure equality under the 1976 Race Relations Act, the 1995 Sex Discrimination Act, and the 1995 Disability Discrimination Act. From the 2000/01 school year they will also be required to meet the requirements of the 1998 Human Rights Act and the Race Relations Amendment Act.

How well does the school work in partnership with parents?

This part of the evaluation schedule has been strengthened. Notably, inspectors are asked to consider the extent to which the school has the confidence of all the parents and communities it serves. One source of evidence is likely to be the OFSTED parents' questionnaire, the other the parents' meeting convened as part of the inspection process. In the questionnaire, parents are asked, for example, whether the school is well led and managed. They are not asked about the degree to which they feel the school promotes equality of opportunity for all pupils, regardless of age, gender, ethnicity, attainment and background, even though this is something inspectors must address.

How well is the school led and managed?

Importantly, in this section, inspectors are asked to consider the extent to which the governing body fulfils its statutory responsibilities with regard to equal opportunities legislation.

Reporting to parents

In the body of the school inspection report, following information about the school and a judgement of how good the school is, inspectors are required to include sections which address

- what the school does well

- what could be improved

- what the school should do to improve further.

The first two sections are recorded in the summary that is made available to parents. These sections are included in the summary report. They replace the sections known as *Main Findings* and *Key Issues for Action*, which were included in the summary report under the previous framework (OFSTED, 1995) and were also made available to parents.

Inspectors' expertise and experience

For all inspections, OFSTED requires inspection team members to have *expertise and experience* which will allow them to inspect efficiently the full age range; all aspects covered in the evaluation schedule; and, where relevant, various stages and aspects of the curriculum. The team must also include one or more inspectors *responsible for* co-ordinating equal opportunities; the education of pupils with special educational needs; where relevant, the education of pupils in the foundation stage; and where relevant, the education of pupils with English as an additional language. It is not clear from *Inspecting Schools* whether an inspector responsible for EAL will be appointed when a school indicates that it has *any* pupils with EAL, or whether there will, in the words of OFSTED, need to be *significant* numbers of such pupils before such a responsibility is designated. Responsibility for an aspect of the curriculum such as equal opportunities or the education of pupils with EAL, does not guarantee expertise or proficiency in that aspect of the curriculum.

Inspection handbooks

The OFSTED framework *Inspecting Schools* is supplemented by three substantial handbooks for primary, secondary and special schools (OFSTED, 1999a, b and c) for use by contracted inspectors and schools, each of which also contains guidance on school self-evaluation. The handbooks generally provide support to schools which are working towards the implementation of stronger inclusion measures. There are, however, some concerns relating to race equality measures, as outlined in the handbooks.

All three handbooks instruct inspectors to examine the information in the PICSI report to find out:

- how well pupils performed in English, mathematics (and where appropriate, science) at various stages in their school careers

- how well pupils attained in one subject as compared with another

- how boys' attainment compares with that of girls.

Inspectors are then required to:

> Discuss with the headteacher of schools serving *more than one significant ethnic minority* group any other significant variation in attainment by different groups of pupils (see, for example, OFSTED 1999b: 29, our emphasis).

This is a curious formulation. According to the handbooks, an inspector looking for evidence at a school with only one 'significant ethnic minority group' among the school population is not required to discuss with the headteacher any significant variation in attainment between this group and the ethnic majority group. So, for example, at a school with 40 per cent African Caribbean and 60 per cent white UK heritage pupils, any variation in attainment between the ethnic minority and ethnic majority group could pass unremarked. It is only when a school has more than one significant ethnic minority group that such a discussion must take place.

The *Handbook for the Inspection of Special Schools* (OFSTED, 1999c) gives minimal guidance on the inspection of provision of English as an additional language. No examples of reports addressing such provision are included. The handbook also fails to provide inspectors with any example of reporting in response to the judgements they are required to make in response to the question: 'Do pupils work in an atmosphere free from oppressive behaviour, such as bullying, sexism and racism?' despite the fact that some children in such schools may be particularly vulnerable to such oppressive behaviour (OFSTED, 1999c: 40).

Conclusion

The Government has given a lead role to OFSTED in the prevention of racism through education. The Government accepted the recommendation of the Stephen Lawrence Inquiry Report that OFSTED inspections include examination of the implementation of strategies to prevent racism in education. Yet it is difficult to see how contracted inspectors will fulfil this duty since neither they nor headteachers have been informed of it. There is no mention of it on the OFSTED website, in circulars to headteachers, or in *Update*, the regular newsletter issued to inspectors. HMCI's Annual Report for 1998-99 made no reference to the Macpherson Report, published earlier that year. Neither did it mention the Government's attribution to OFSTED of a lead role in preventing racism through education.

The current inspection framework, which came into operation in January 2000, has a number of additional features which have the potential to contribute to greater racial equality in schools. It adopts the term 'educational inclusion' to cover a range of equality issues, including race equality. Yet this document, and most of the other material issued by OFSTED, fails to discuss racism or its impact on learners, whether these learners are from minority or majority ethnic communities.

OFSTED's failure to name and discuss racism and 'openly and adequately to recognise and address its existence and causes by policy, example and leadership' places OFSTED, and its contracted inspectors, in a weak position to fulfil the lead role given to it by Government. It is difficult to see how OFSTED and its leadership can contribute effectively and decisively to the prevention of racism through the inspection of schools while OFSTED continues to avoid explicit discussion of racism in its policy documents and public statements.

Note

1. See Appendix item 3 for correspondence between Audrey Osler and Her Majesty's Chief Inspector of Schools which sought to clarify this issue.

Chapter 3

HMI PERSPECTIVES ON RACE EQUALITY AND SCHOOL INSPECTION

Our original research proposal, agreed with OFSTED, invited Her Majesty's Chief Inspector to contribute to the research by way of an interview. Unfortunately, two requests for an interview with HMCI, the second by the Chief Executive of the Commission for Racial Equality, were both declined on the grounds that the Chief Inspector was too busy to meet the research team. However, HMCI proposed that we meet instead two other members of the OFSTED senior management team with responsibility for school inspections. A third member of HMI accompanied them during the ensuing interview.

Interviews with senior OFSTED personnel took place between November 1999 and January 2000. We interviewed three members of the OFSTED senior management team and three other members of HMI, including individuals with the following roles and responsibilities: the management of school inspection; the development of the new inspection framework; experts in 'educational inclusion' and in the teaching and learning of English as an additional language (EAL).

The final set of interviews, which we report on below, consisted of:

- two individual interviews with members of HMI

- an individual interview with a member of the senior management team

- a group interview which included two members of the senior management team and a third member of HMI.

These interviews provided us with a rich source of data, addressing, among other things:

- the two inspection frameworks

- the processes of inspection

- personal understandings of race equality in education

- OFSTED's role in preventing racism through education.

Inspection frameworks and race equality

Views of the current and former frameworks

We discussed with members of HMI the potential of the 2000 framework to support race equality initiatives in schools. One member of HMI suggested that it is, in general terms, much stronger than the previous framework because it is now drafted as a series of questions and this encourages inspectors to make sharper judgements and move away from any tendency to be merely descriptive:

> There is a radical shift in terms of much greater evaluation. The framework itself, instead of being a series of headings is now phrased as evaluative questions.

However, another pointed out that the old framework (1996-99) had been a valuable tool, capable of being used by inspectors to support and assess a range of equality initiatives:

> I've always felt that the actual framework was relatively robust. In other words there were plenty of prompts in it that as a Registered Inspector, reporting inspector or attached inspector, you could use, providing you had the knowledge and the experience. There was plenty of opportunity to look at differential attainment by minority ethnic group, to look at issues such as racial harassment and so on. The prompts were all there. ... I'm quite sure it was robust enough to enable a good inspection and a good report to be produced around equalities issues, not least because there are (some) very good reports.

The key issue for this member of HMI was not the quality of the previous framework but the quality of the contracted inspectors and, in particular, the commitment of the reporting inspector to questions of equality. This inspector argued that even if there were team members who were sensitive to race equality issues and who observed and examined their development in the school, such issues were not necessarily included in the final report unless the reporting inspector judged them to be significant:

> The key person was the reporting inspector, and if that person didn't choose to take on board some of those comments, or didn't see their significance or didn't feel they were specific issues for that school, then even though they may have been looked at within a process of inspection, they may not have featured in the final report. So yes, that person is absolutely key, a bit like a headteacher in a school. And if that person doesn't have a vision around equalities issues then there may be patches of good practice but the school as a whole won't actually take them on board and get them into its sort of systems and routines.

As a member of the OFSTED senior management team acknowledged:

> [OFSTED] set out a framework for inspection within which inspectors have considerable discretion in terms of operating it. The fundamental point of inspection is that it is the art of the possible and what inspectors have to do is to not only evaluate how things are but make particular mention in reports if there are real strengths or weaknesses in the school. Therefore, I think, if one is looking at the outcomes of inspection in [a report], first of all, inspectors would not at that stage have necessarily made reference to racial or ethnicity issues even in a multi-ethnic school if there were no issues.

Thus race equality issues are likely to be overlooked unless there are perceived problems or particular strengths which the reporting inspector judges to be worth mentioning.

Nevertheless, members of HMI placed considerable faith in the capacity of the current (2000) framework to permit the monitoring of equality initiatives in schools more effectively than was possible under the previous framework:

> I think that there is little doubt that in my mind that, particularly in the new framework, there are things that work that were implicit which are made much more explicit. We have better tools to make demands both on the inspectors and, indirectly, of schools. I am sure that the new

framework actually sets out a notional model of good practice – certainly good management practice – which I think I am certain. I mean, this is a speculation on my part, but I believe that it will make a major contribution to greater awareness and greater effective management and responses to those [equality] issues where they are significant in schools. ... Heads will know and will act if there is evidence of differential achievement, whether it be in terms of attainment or behaviour when youngsters arrive in the school. There is an expectation on reporting, particularly incidents relating to sexual or racial harassment. Which is of course supported now by the requirements from the DfEE circulars. And lastly, particularly where schools are in receipt of additional funding of any sort – programme funding whether it be from EMTAG or whatever – where that money is going into the schools for specific purposes which may include meeting the needs of particular youngsters – ... that that money is accounted for and, in very strict terms, that it is evaluated and monitored.

Ethnic monitoring

I think we have learned three things since the 1996 inspection [framework]. We have learned that we must know a lot more about the characteristics of schools; we have learned that teaching is of the essence; and we have learned that the management is the key to how schools do well. *Member of HMI.*

One particular feature of the new framework that members of HMI feel will encourage inspectors to look more closely at differential attainment, is the emphasis placed on ethnic composition in describing the characteristics of the schools. This, together with the requirement, when judging standards and assessing teaching, to look at the outcomes for different groups of pupils, is what they believe will make a difference.

Yet HMI recognises that there is still a long way to go in encouraging schools and LEAs to develop adequate systems of ethnic monitoring. Referring to the old framework, one member of HMI commented:

That first section [reporting on the characteristics of the school] was often very poorly done, often quite unacceptable terminology as well. That, for me, very often was an indication of what might come later on in the report. Because if it was not very clear what the report context

42

was, it very rarely subsequently became clear within the report itself, what was being talked about.

Another observed that certain ethnic groups were often invisible in reports:

> We found that we had not done enough to bring out the element that we were concerned about, about invisibility and things disappearing in the old framework, and particularly in the characteristics of the school. ...It will no longer be possible to get to page 50 of a report and realise you have got a large proportion of Black Caribbean boys in a school. It is going to be up front now in the characteristics of the school.

Yet inspectors are still dependent on schools to provide them with adequate data from which they can make judgements about the differential experiences of various groups. There are a number of steps to go between providing a helpful description of a school which describes its ethnic composition and developing a sensitive system of monitoring by ethnicity which is followed up by specific actions to address any inequalities in provision. A deeper understanding of the potential of ethnic monitoring across the whole education community is needed, if it is to be used as a tool to enhance standards in education. Schools will need more support in this area than many are currently receiving from their LEAs. As another member of HMI noted:

> We found in the report I referred to earlier, *Raising the Attainment of Minority Ethnic Pupils,* only a third of LEAs have what we found to be acceptable comprehensive data [on attainment] with respect to the minority ethnic groups in their LEAs.

As another inspector pointed out, the reporting on the attainment of ethnic minority pupils in inspected schools does not correspond to the national picture. This would suggest that contracted inspectors have not had data which would allow them to make accurate assessments of the relative performance of different groups within a school:

> We had a kind of disjunction of message. Reports seem to be indicating that things were OK and yet, against that, performance data on youngsters from different ethnic minorities actually showed a different picture. ... The inspectors were at the mercy of inadequate monitoring

by schools, performance data, ethnicity, that is a rapidly changing picture. [Inspectors] actually didn't really have the data tools to do the job. We're saying, you know, they could perceive that, the phrase is burned in my mind because I've read it that often, *There are no differences in attainment between ethnic groups.*' ... If it is true then this is a remarkable institution because it, at an individual level, it is acting against all the trends that appear from national data.

A member of the OFSTED senior management team concluded that the responsibility for ethnic monitoring rests with the school:

There is the access or the lack of access to data at school level and that clearly has been a significant difficulty. We can't help the problem because we are receiving pupil level information and cannot in any way identify the ethnic background of the pupils. So we can't do much by way of helping the inspectors, it has got to be at the school level and many schools have not got as far, for whatever reasons. I am not suggesting anything sinister or significant. In some schools they do not even do it for boys versus girls, never mind anything more radical than that in their thinking.

Another senior manager noted that, by adopting a colour-blind approach, some contracting inspectors might fail to highlight examples of good practice in raising the achievement of ethnic minority pupils. He highlighted an example from his personal experience:

I visited a school inspection in C, which had a large group of children who were from African Caribbean background. And I was there at the final team meeting of very experienced inspectors in a very good school. It was a high achieving primary school and the black children were achieving just as highly as the white children in that school. Fantastic ethos, it was actually a Roman Catholic school and there was in the discussion, it was clear, that it would be unlikely that there would be anything in the report that remarked on the fact that despite the school serving two different ethnic communities, in that sense, achievement was remarkably high and indistinguishably good across all the children as a whole. I just made a comment, 'Do you think it's worth a mention? What's the secret?' But because there was no problem or no issue, the report was sort of sailing to a happy conclusion and the team just didn't think that it was worth mentioning.

An appropriate curriculum

Another weakness recognised in the old inspection framework was its lack of guidance on what constitutes an appropriate curriculum, providing equality of access for all:

> [Inspectors'] interpretation of the curriculum very often was at the level of 'Had the school given any thought at all about the use of materials that might be stereotypical?' So there would be some sort of comment about the library having looked at its stock with these issues in mind. You did see it occasionally in reports, comments to the effect that the curriculum took little account of the broader cultural needs, not only in this country, but [also] internationally. ...There was rarely any reporting that indicated that an entire school had taken the whole look right across its curriculum and ordered it from a race equality perspective. ...Very rarely did each inspector looking at separate subjects actually address that question within his or her own subject specialism.

Again, examples of good practice may be overlooked.

One member of HMI felt that it was unlikely that questions of race equality would be identified for inspection under the current arrangements, beyond what inspectors already look for in the context of 'pupils' spiritual, moral, social and cultural development', until Citizenship Education is introduced nationally in 2002:

> We have got new National Curriculum documents ... all the stuff on Citizenship ... will also be a dimension in which you would expect to see the kinds of things you're interested in reflected. That is not something we can inspect yet.

Monitoring the teaching of English as an additional language

It was recognised that inspectors' understanding of teaching English as an additional language has been especially weak. It is only since 1998 that EAL specialists are eligible to apply to be inspectors:

> I think it would be true to say that it has been quite difficult for those who actually know about teaching EAL to have got into the inspection process in the first place, partly because they were seen as marginal, on the edges. They didn't fit the criteria [to qualify as an inspector]. ... If you don't actually know a subject in great detail you tend to see things as much better than they actually might be, partly because you don't

actually know what constitutes good practice. And therefore you see something going on which looks organised and well thought out and planned, there's a tendency to assume that maybe that's good practice. So I would say that reporting on EAL has not been of the quality that it should have been. ...EAL is now recognised as an area within the inspection process. That was changed about eighteen months ago, and so people with that qualification can put themselves forward.

Others shared this viewpoint. For example:

If, within your question, you are saying that some of the reporting, some of these issues like EAL doesn't seem to be sufficiently penetrating or whatever, then yeah we'd agree with you. We'd have no difficulty with that. You know they are searching to improve all the time and there are weaker areas in inspections. The weaker areas tend to be the areas that are rather harder to get at and to get evidence for.

Nevertheless, it is questionable whether it should be more difficult to find evidence on the teaching of EAL rather than, say, mathematics, if appropriate inspectors are appointed to carry out this task. It would appear that the difficulty lies in the expertise of contracted inspectors, rather than in the availability of evidence. As we have noted in chapter two, the current framework requires only that an individual inspector takes *responsibility* for EAL when there are a significant number of EAL learners. It does not assume, or require, that the responsible inspector has any *expertise* in the area.

Racial harassment

One of the four points in OFSTED's formal response to the recommendations of the Macpherson Report, as reported in the Government's action plan, is to monitor the new anti-bullying guidance issued by the DfEE (1999) as part of its regular programme of school inspection (Home Office, 2000). One member of HMI argued that, first, it is extremely difficult to establish through the processes of regular inspections whether or not racial harassment is taking place in a school and that, secondly, inspectors needed to develop their skills in this area:

I actually find all of these things are quite difficult to get at in inspection, I mean the kind of inspection that goes on in the week-long [Section 10] inspection. Certainly we've done a lot of work, HMI this is, on focused inspections that we've looked at things like racial harassment and how schools respond to that, and *we find it actually takes a lot of time to get underneath what might appear on the surface to be good relationships*. ... So the kind of things you need to do is talk to the kids in an informal, unthreatening situation. ...There are schools that have excellent procedures in place for racial harassment and how you handle it, and other forms of harassment and that's simply an area that schools need to develop as well as inspectors, in terms of their ability to inspect that (our emphasis).

As HMI acknowledge, pupils are thus a crucial source of evidence for this aspect of inspection. Any training programme on educational inclusion and racial equality would therefore need to address how such evidence might best be collected without causing pupils at risk of harassment to be placed at additional risk.

Racial harassment can also be tackled directly through the curriculum, and this, too, can be addressed in inspection, as a member of HMI highlighted:

Yes, I mean what people were looking at was whether there was anything in the PSHE [Personal, Social and Health Education] programmes that would counter things like discrimination, racism, stereotyping, and also the equality of relationships, which as I have said, it is very easy to get completely the wrong view about how good relationships are just sitting looking at the classroom. It often requires a lot more digging underneath to be able to say genuinely that race equality is fine in a school. I mean my own experience in inspecting in this area is that nearly always youngsters, like minority ethnic youngsters, suffer some form of racial harassment, discrimination, almost on a daily basis, whether it is on the way to school, whether it is at school, through gesture, it might be other pupils, it might be remarks from teachers, or whatever. It may be in terms of actually which sets they are in. There is a myriad of issues that you actually need to measure to be quite sure that the school genuinely is serving all its pupils fairly, and very hard to get at. I don't think that section ever really got very much below the surface and I actually think it's quite hard to do so. ... The straightforward weekly inspection was probably not the kind of inspection that would be able to get underneath some of those race issues.

This individual is questioning whether Section 10 inspections, as currently formulated, are able to address race equality issues satisfactorily.

Relationships with parents and the community

One member of HMI pointed out that although the emphasis is largely on attainment and on issues relating to relationships within a school, there are other indicators of race equality in a school. Some of these are overlooked because of the focus of school inspections, and also because of a lack of awareness on the part of some contracted inspectors:

> But there are other indicators, aren't there, it's not just the issue of actual racial harassment and the relationships, it's about relationships with the parents and the wider community, and all sorts of things you need to do which will be different if you are from a white school, a school which has large numbers of minority ethnic groups or whatever.

Overview

Most members of HMI whom we interviewed were confident that the current framework would make a more substantial contribution to race equality than the former one:

> These documents, I think, shift the ground of inspection significantly from good intentions to requirements that are going to be more rigorously and more effectively scrutinised and implemented.

Yet no reports based on the current inspection framework were available at the time of these interviews:

> We've actually yet to see the reports being written under the new framework. My own guess is that it will be just the same as the one before. That where you've got an inspection team or a reporting inspector who is strong on these issues, there is absolutely nothing there that will prevent you from writing a cracking report that teases these things out. But there's no doubt that there is still a lot more work that needs to be done in terms of training for teams generally and OFSTED has recognised that also and is planning to do that.

While the current framework is an improvement in many ways on the previous one, its effectiveness in terms of enabling race equality is likely to depend largely on the processes of reporting. These, in turn,

are likely to depend upon the opportunities for trai
race equality provided to contracted inspectors by O

Educational inclusion

The term 'educational inclusion' has been introduced in the current
framework. It was summarised by one member of HMI as follows:

> Now that is an umbrella title that does contain much more than racial
> equality. But that's a fundamental part that I don't think any inspectors
> using the new framework could go into a school and not come away
> with a view of the way in which different groups of pupils have achieved
> and are achieving, and are being taught and the standards they are
> reaching.

OFSTED's use of the term educational inclusion covers, as we have
seen in chapter 2, race and gender equality, special educational needs,
the teaching of English as an additional language and the needs of
gifted pupils. A member of HMI explained that the development of the
framework had taken place within the context of Government
initiatives in education which focus on both standards and inclusion:

> We were conscious when designing this framework that we needed to
> take note both of wider political Government initiatives of the DfEE on
> the whole, issues about achievement and social inclusion, but also *in
> catching the spirit of the times* (our emphasis).

This interviewee made several references to the 'spirit of the times'
which we understand to refer to the wider public and media awareness
of the need to ensure race equality and to the Government's commitment to this goal, following the publication early in 1999 of the
Stephen Lawrence Inquiry Report.

Educational inclusion was primarily understood by our interviewees to
refer to ensuring that all pupils, regardless of their social or cultural
backgrounds, reach high academic standards:

> We have got the concept of achievement and the concept of attainment.
> Attainment is matched against pupil levels. Achievement is matched
> against more or less capabilities. Is this school getting everything it can
> out of these pupils? So the concept of achievement which you will find

> here [in the new framework] is an important other source of evidence to make sure the school is extending all its pupils.

These concepts of attainment and achievement are of particular importance in relation to the realisation of racial equality in schools. Attainment relates directly to national curriculum levels and the degree to which pupils at 7, 11, 14 and 16 years meet or exceed national standards in their tests. Judgements of educational standards 'should be based on the extent to which ... the attainment and progress of minority groups of pupils is comparable with others in the school' (OFSTED, 1999b: 16).

The member of HMI matches achievement with 'capabilities'. This raises a question about how capabilities might be assessed. Inspectors are advised that achievement:

> *reflects the accomplishments of pupils in relation to what you would expect of those particular pupils.* There are few clear reference points. Reference to terms such as 'ability' or 'aptitude' requires caution, for it is questionable what evidence you will have of such attributes. Prior attainment is a more secure judgement, if it has been measured, but essentially *you should judge achievement by applying insight and expertise to all the evidence you have about the pupils,* taking account of what they know, understand and can do, and what they are being asked to do. Broader indicators, such as *measures which compare standards with those in similar schools and value added measures, are also helpful* in indicating the relative progress of pupils and providing a clue to how well they are achieving (OFSTED, 1999b: 23, our emphasis).

This definition has important implications for the realisation of race equality in schools. Inspectors are required to judge achievement according to their expectations ('what you would expect of those particular pupils') and to use their own insights, since 'there are few clear reference points'. Thus the concept of achievement appears more subjective than that of attainment. A reliance on inspector expectations raises some concerns, bearing in mind the evidence we have of low teacher expectations of pupils from certain ethnic minority communities (for example, see Gillborn and Gipps, 1996). Inspectors are also advised to compare standards with those of similar schools. If comparisons are made with schools with a similar ethnic profile and with attainment levels below national norms, then it is difficult to see how higher expectations of pupils from these minority communities might be encouraged.

One member of HMI hoped that the new framework would avoid confusion between terms such as equal opportunities, ethnic diversity and EAL:

> It became common practice to equate, in many instances, issues of ethnic diversity with youngsters who have English as additional language. Somehow the measure of diversity was seen to be the same as English as an additional language. ... So often when you read reports the thinking seemed to move between EAL provision for youngsters with English as additional language as being the same as the school's response to issues of ethnic diversity. And they are, in a sense, quite separate issues.

Our analysis of inspection reports (see chapter five) confirms that, under the previous framework, EAL and race equality often became conflated in the process of reporting. The member of HMI being interviewed went on to suggest that this is because one person took on the responsibility for inspecting both equal opportunities and EAL. Yet the current framework also allows one inspector to take on multiple responsibilities in this area, as before, without the need for any expertise in any of them.

Other members of HMI pointed out that whatever the terminology employed, the realisation of race equality in schools depended on the commitment of the school's senior management:

> There is no way that the whole of the school's processes and procedures will actually be taken on and scrutinised and altered, unless the senior management address those issues as a central tenet of what is important about that school. Again, in the good examples that we came up with it was always the case that the headteacher or the senior management gave a lead in this area.

> If an indicator of a successful school means that it educates positively for full racial equality and it expects that to be not only attitudinal but also to be there in terms of what children do, what they take away with them, and the way the whole of the school relates to that community, then that is all management.

51

A question of evidence

It was pointed out to us by a number of members of OFSTED that one of the difficulties in reporting on race equality matters was difficulty in finding evidence:

> [It] will come through the management questions that are asked about 'Where is the evidence?' and 'Why not?' Now the inspectors cannot invent the evidence if the school has got no record of this. Your pre-inspection commentary, which is very important, which identifies issues for your team, will ensure that you cover those things in your inspection.

> I think you are right to be sceptical. I think that the sections on spiritual, moral, social and cultural are not the best. ... They can be easily impressionistic, easy to come over with soft answers. I think it depends upon the proper co-ordination of evidence of an inspection team, and the alertness in an inspection team to what is spiritual, social, moral and cultural. It depends on the quality of inspections going on in classrooms and the quality of the evidence.

One inspector concluded that the way in which educational inclusion is understood and the degree of prominence that race equality receives within inspection is largely dependent on the wider political climate and on the attention given by Government to race equality:

> Maybe someone will say we need to review post the next election. Possibly a second term of office for a Labour Government. We'll need to think again.

Inspection processes

We understand that HMI reviews a sample of school inspection reports annually and that it should be possible to review reports completed under the current framework to assess whether they are dealing more effectively with equality issues than has been the case in the past:

> What we do is review reports formally. We review a third, or 25 per cent to a third, every year and our reviewing will take note of the quality of reporting all these equal opportunities.

Short inspections

One issue we wished to explore with members of HMI was whether, under the new arrangements for short inspections, contracting inspectors would be able to identify issues of race equality when they spend a short period in a school:

> We hope that it won't miss anything. The nature of a short inspection is very different. The selection of schools for 'light touch' should mean that they are achieving high standards with all the pupils they have got.

The question of whether schools identified for short inspections are actually achieving high standards for *all* pupils, remains difficult to assess. As we have seen, OFSTED readily admits that the ethnic monitoring process has in many cases been inadequate, thus denying inspectors access to data which would allow them to state with any degree of accuracy that a school is achieving high standards for all.

Reporting

In interviewing members of HMI, we were anxious to understand why most of them believed that the concept of 'educational inclusion' might better support race equality in schools than 'equal opportunities' had done under the previous framework. One member of HMI explained that under the old framework the concept of equal opportunities had become confused with EAL by contracted inspectors. It was argued that, by adopting the new terminology, the needs of certain minority groups who had previously been overlooked because of this conceptual confusion would now be addressed. It would also be helpful that the reporting inspector could now choose how to describe the school in terms of ethnicity without having to negotiate this description with the headteacher and governing body:

> [The] issue is really to do with inspection reporting. Sometimes there is a subtlety which is lost and needs to be remembered. That under all previous inspection frameworks the description of the school is a matter that was expected to be agreed between the inspector and headteacher and governing body and under the new framework not, because it is now solely the responsibility of the inspector to describe the school's characteristics. Now that ... resulted in many schools, and descriptions of schools, literally losing issues to do with characterising the school in

terms of minority ethnic groups. ...The group which was most often disappeared ... was often the African Caribbean and African pupils. ... And
the second group were Travellers. And I think the issue in relation to
Travellers presents many more difficulties. And I can think of one classic
example of where, in our sample, we read a report where it's not clear
until two thirds of the way through that there were Travellers that were
mentioned. And yet actually it was a school which had clearly identified
its responsibilities, it involved the Traveller Education Service ...Yet it was
actually as much as 25 per cent of that particular school's intake was
from a Traveller background.

It was explained to the researcher that sometimes schools did not wish
to highlight particular minority groups such as Travellers in the school
population for fear of attracting adverse publicity or hostility within
the local community. Members of HMI argued that some headteachers
felt this might undermine the positive work that was taking place with
pupils.

Matching needs

A member of the OFSTED senior management team explained the
steps that had been taken to recruit contracted inspectors from a range
of ethnic groups, so that inspectors could be more appropriately
'matched' to the schools they are inspecting:

I mean we tried hard at one time; we do not have sufficient inspectors
from ethnic minority groups. We have tried very, very hard even to the
point of selective adverts; even advice on placing adverts in the ethnic
minority press. We have to report that we have some weak [applicants?]
... We have to regard that we have far, far fewer than we ideally would
like. And, I mean, often our contractors, for example, would like to have
access to give the right bent to the team. In a sense that is an issue for
us. All the efforts that have been made so far have not given us the
product we would have liked.

An example was given of one particularly striking under-representation:

I can give you quite a specific example. In 10,000 inspectors, say, I can
only find four who are Bengali speakers.

Special measures

We were keen to understand whether, in the eyes of members of HMI, a school might be placed in special measures as a result of race inequality. Under the previous framework schools could be judged to have serious weaknesses or require special measures. Under the current framework a third category is created of 'underachieving' schools. A member of the senior management team confirmed:

> A school can be declared to be in special measures simply on the fact that behaviour and relationships have broken down. And in so far as that is true, those behaviours and relationships may well be ones of a nature that are showing racial harassment or racial abuse or whatever. So I mean, that alone would trigger special measures whereas, if you like, standards alone might not.

This point was qualified by another inspector who pointed out:

> Well, not even there, because the new guidance says if there is an identifiable group of pupils whose performance is consistently below the rest that is sufficient.

However, another inspector was more sceptical:

> I think that the weighting [on decisions relating to special measures] tends to go to things like management, standards, the underachievement and the curriculum. ... So I guess that even if it was something you were concerned about, it may be indicated on the report, although *not many of them actually do indicate them* [race equality issues] *as major issues or key issues*.

This last comment confirms our findings. In the sample of inspection reports we studied (see chapter five) there is no evidence that race equality issues, even when they were identified as significant, were highlighted as key issues for action by a school.

Individuals' understandings of race equality in education

We found a wide range of understandings of race equality issues in education among members of HMI. Two of our six interviewees were of the belief that any approach to race equality in education and in school inspection should be explicit, recognising that we have yet to achieve a society where racial equality has been realised:

I think many things need to be explicit. My personal view is that ... there is no point doing things by stealth. ... The wider social values and tolerance should be reflected in the expectations of the school. I can't say our society is terribly tolerant but that is another matter. But I would expect the school in that sense to be a microcosm of what goes on in society in general. And just as, if you live in an all white area, you have to know that all people are equal, so even if you are in an all white school, so the focus on bullying, the focus on opportunities, the focus on relationships in any school ought to be quite clear. Both because there is a legacy of racial discrimination, indeed racial prejudice and racial hatred in our society willy nilly, and I think that our schools have got to counteract that positively.

The following dialogue between two members of the OFSTED senior management team reflects a rather different perspective, where race equality appears to be viewed as an add-on, rather than a fundamental aspect of the promotion and maintenance of high standards in schools:

HMI 1   There is also a tension about how much of the Section framework, and we have often used the expression here about: 'hanging baubles on the Christmas tree until the thing topples over'. And if every possible group and every possible interest which bears on education wants their thing represented in the framework, whether it is the Asthmatic Society or whether it is a major issue to do with the EOC or CRE or, you know, it is parents' issues or it is you know, promoting family life. We have, across my desk, almost at certain times of year, several who wish these sorts of claims for inclusion. And inspectors must report on their experience, why on earth aren't they?

HMI 2   The framework has become a point, almost a value offer. If you are in it and you are interested in it you have really arrived. And it means that it has more importance than those matters which aren't in it. And I mean, if we allowed ourselves to be blown by every group who wanted to be a piece of the sum we would have a framework which more or less changed every month and grown to a volume which is enormous. So there is a limit that we have to impose.

HMI 1   Having said that though we recognise the importance and the centrality of yours.

HMI 2   Oh, the centrality and legal obligations of the schools, that's right.

Promoting race equality in white schools

Among senior personnel at OFSTED there was acknowledgement of the particular difficulties that predominantly white schools might face in promoting race equality. Nevertheless, it was acknowledged that such schools needed to demonstrate that they have in place a curriculum which recognises diversity in our society and promotes co-operation and understanding:

> Having worked a lot in places like N [a largely rural district] rather than in multi-ethnic schools, city schools. There is no doubt about it. Getting children and often long-standing staff to see cultural diversity and cultural issues as important is an uphill battle.

> That fact that we have to look at the social, moral, spiritual and cultural development of pupils, we do see, within that, as [it has] got to be inspected. I think I would say that the fact that it is an all-white school ... one would challenge it very strongly. ... [Pupils] may have to interact [with others from diverse backgrounds] if they move school or jobs or whatever. ... That they don't see any need to do that, is arguing on the basis of 'Why should we, because we don't have...?' and our argument is 'No, you don't, but your children that you are looking at, live in that diverse cultural society.' ... And they should have an understanding and appreciation of it even though they don't have ethnic minority representation in their school.

Members of HMI acknowledged racism in the community as something which schools in both disadvantaged and advantaged communities might have to face. They pointed out that education alone was unlikely to be effective in challenging racism:

> Our schools are you know, city schools battling every week against, you know, the racism in the football ground on the Saturday, you know, schools and the national curriculum and inspections can only do so much. And I mean you are far more aware, I am sure, than I am but when you have got an indigenous racism in the community around the school you know, the school has in some cases an uphill battle. When you have got very comfortable ... and gentle sort of community around them in rural areas which are monocultural so it is all very complex. But I think what we are expecting inspectors to do is to go in there and we expect them themselves to reflect good practice in their behaviour and the way they think about schools and the needs of young people. To go in there with their eyes open.

The role of OFSTED in preventing racism through education

In our interviews with HMI we sought to understand how they understand the lead role which the Government has given OFSTED in preventing racism through education. Members of OFSTED had varied
understandings of the actual and potential role school inspection might
play in contributing to the prevention of racism through education.
One senior inspector suggested that:

> In fairness, the job of making the schools more sensitive or responsive
> to this cannot be laid solely at the door of the inspectorate. And there
> is a great danger of doing that. The fact is that the inspection of most
> schools is an event that will take place once every three years or there-
> abouts.

Others saw the prevention of racism through education as something
which has to be attempted, not simply to address disadvantage and dis-
parity between ethnic groups but for the future benefit of all members
of society. In that sense OFSTED could be seen as contributing to a
more widespread effort to rid society of race inequality:

> It is not only OFSTED. I think the DfEE are much more interested than
> they were, and I think it's the spirit of the times. It's all a sort of social
> feeling. You can ignore these things at our peril, and I think we have been
> part of that.

But not all shared this viewpoint. One member of the senior management team informed us:

> Race equality is not a priority. Our priority is underachieving white boys.

While the priority given to white boys was specifically denied by
HMCI (see Appendix item 3), we have found no evidence that race
equality is a particular priority for the inspection service. When asked
about the priority given to race equality in OFSTED, one HMI told us:

> I don't think race equality is [a priority] per se, I think equality of oppor-
> tunity is. So all I would do is broaden the umbrella. ... The new frame-
> work reflects it [educational inclusion] and there is a lot of energy and
> a lot of expertise in OFSTED. I think we take it seriously and I believe it
> is at the heart of school community. What I think we would say is that
> it seems to us to be bigger than just a race equality issue, but the issue
> of how to achieve, how well they are taught.

Interviews with other members of the OFSTED senior management team lead us to question whether they were, in fact, aware of the lead role of preventing racism through education assigned to OFSTED by Government. Since we knew of no public documents issued by OFSTED outlining this role, we wrote to Her Majesty's Chief Inspector of Schools, asking him if he would provide us with any documents which draw the attention of HMI to the role of OFSTED School Inspection in the Home Secretary's Action Plan. Since this plan states that 'OFSTED ... will ensure that the important issues raised in the (Macpherson) report are addressed during inspections' we also asked if he would provide us with a copy of any letter or memorandum sent to HMI, registered inspectors or headteachers concerning this. We were informed by HMCI that:

> We do not rely on paper communication in OFSTED. Important issues are always a matter for discussion in division meetings. *Correspondence from HMCI, 1 March 2000.*

A copy of HMCI's letter is included as Appendix item 3. Although we are led to believe that OFSTED's role in the prevention of racism might be discussed in an HMI divisional meeting, no minute or other record of such a meeting has been made available to us, despite our request for such evidence (see correspondence from Audrey Osler to Chris Woodhead, dated 18 February 2000: Appendix item 3). It is not clear to us whether this matter has been discussed in all divisions of OFSTED or how anyone who was not present at a relevant meeting would learn about the lead role assigned to OFSTED by Government. Neither do we have any evidence to suggest that headteachers have been been informed by OFSTED of the Government's responding to Macpherson in March 1999 by assigning a lead role to OFSTED in preventing racism in and through education. A Spring 2000 edition of *Update*, the publication for inspectors, mentions the new emphasis on educational inclusion, but it is not clear from this that race equality is central to the concept:

> Inspecting Schools places greater and sharper emphasis on educational inclusion when schools are inspected. Previous inspection Frameworks required inspectors to report on the performance and progress of *different groups of pupils.* Inspectors are now required to identify whether

any children are excluded from making full use of the available opportunities offered by schools and evaluate the reasons for this. They must evaluate how effective are the efforts made by schools to overcome *barriers to pupils' full participation in learning* (OFSTED, 2000b, our emphasis).

While 'different groups of pupils' may include groupings by ethnicity, this is not explicit. And while 'barriers to pupils' full participation in learning' may be interpreted as including such things as racial harassment, discrimination and stereotyping, this is not spelt out, and again the language is imprecise. There is no reference in this definition of educational inclusion to more positive concepts, such as equality and justice. In order to try and understand why OFSTED has chosen to express the concept of educational inclusion in this way, it is worth focusing on how HMI understand the language of race equality and on the use of language within OFSTED.

A common language

One member of HMI felt that the term 'race equality' had not been commonly used within the organisation but that the issues of race equality remained key ones for schools:

> I think race equality was probably not a phrase that we were using at that point. I mean it was equal opportunities, wasn't it? And racial harassment. Race equality and racial justice is really within the last year or two [that it] has become much more widely used.

Members of OFSTED drew our attention to the importance of language issues in relation to equalities in education. In particular they cited the series of OFSTED national curriculum pamphlets produced in February 1999, which included, in the secondary series, one relating to Equal Opportunities. This provides guidance on equal opportunities in relation to the previous inspection framework. It addresses attainment and progress; attitudes, behaviour, personal development and attendance; teaching; curriculum and assessment; leadership and management; and issues relating to particular groups. It stresses that 'The Framework applies to all pupils in the school' and instructs inspectors of equal opportunities:

> to report on the attainment and progress of different groups of pupils, highlighting where the schools' provision does not match all pupils' needs. You judge how effective the school is in raising standards, or maintaining them when they are high, and in promoting good personal, community and race relations. You evaluate the extent to which the school provides equal opportunities for all its pupils to learn and make progress (OFSTED, 1999e: 1).

Under the heading 'minority ethnic groups, including refugees', the pamphlet goes on to mention the needs of ethnic minority parents, the wider community, local services and agencies to support minority and refugee pupils. It requires inspectors of equal opportunities to evaluate the effectiveness of specific grant funding to support minorities. It instructs inspectors to find out whether there is sexual or racial harassment, noting that evidence may come from parents, school records and behaviour around the school. It does not suggest that pupils themselves might give evidence directly to inspectors. Although it refers inspectors to the appropriate legislation, it does not use the terms racial discrimination, racism or race equality. There is no equivalent equal opportunities pamphlet published in the OFSTED national curriculum series for primary schools and no explanation of this imbalance.

Another HMI felt that there has been some uncertainty in schools about the appropriate language to use when discussing race equality, among both teachers and inspectors:

> I absolutely am sure that, through contact with the schools and inspectors, that in part there have been for a long time a lack of confidence to be able to talk about differences in attainment and behaviour of different ethnic groups. Well, I think that it is lack of language and people coming into the school who themselves... *there hasn't been in a sense an apparent common language to which all the inspectors of the schools have access to.* And part of the evolution and development of data has actually been the growing consensus about actually how groups would be identified and spoken about (our emphasis).

This viewpoint was shared by a member of the senior management team:

> I think it is language. I think it's also confidence. I think part of the lack of confidence in some cases comes from any lack of hard information or data so, I mean, a good inspector, and we would insist on this, will not make judgements in the absence of sufficient data to back up that judgement.

The development of a 'common language to which all the inspectors have access' is unlikely to be achieved if HMI and its leadership do not themselves begin to use a language of race equality. The lack of such a language, and the lack of confidence in using it, highlights the need for training and discussion of the topic so as to help inspectors find the right words.

Training and awareness raising

Our discussions with members of HMI confirmed that contracted inspectors have never been issued with specific guidance or instruction on equalities in the OFSTED publication *Update*, which is issued several times a year and highlights key issues for consideration during inspection.

We learned, however, that contracted inspectors are likely to be given mandatory training in 'educational inclusion'. This is confirmed in the first review of the Government's action plan in response to Macpherson (Home Office, 2000). According to HMI, this training is to be based on the document *Educational Inclusion* (OFSTED, 2000b) and provided by distance learning:

> Now, you will be aware that under a new framework the term 'equal opportunities' is not dropped, but it is now subsumed within the notion that we have, which is called 'educational inclusion', right? ... I mean we have produced ... for more wider circulation a paper on educational inclusion and school inspection. And that will be the basis of the compulsory distance training package.

> To be able to unpack the term which we have used, which is educational inclusion, which of itself is made up of quite a number of different [features] and not just within OFSTED, about equal opportunities and some equality legislation which I think has somehow not always been clear. I think even the inspectors might not have a clue what the social inclusion is and what the social exclusion is. ... The framework ...

translates all those pressures into an educational context and focuses around those parts that inspectors do need in inspection.

I think it is a big element is being able to create a training programme which allows people to identify gaps in their knowledge in an OK way, whether it be on issues of gender or in some cases to do with ethnic minorities, or Travellers or EAL that they don't understand. And they need to be brought up to speed. And I think that the training programme that we certainly have planned, and we are well down the track with that, addresses all those needs. It is going to be a demanding programme to implement simply because of the scope of concerns that fall under the term 'educational inclusion' of which race equality is one.

As we have seen in chapter two, such training has since been confirmed in the Spring 2000 issue of *Update*, although it is not clear whether all inspectors will be required to undergo such training since OFSTED only states that 'participation is *likely* to be mandatory' (OFSTED, 2000b: 17 our emphasis). Given the large numbers of personnel involved, a distance learning package seems the only realistic training option. Distance learning alone is unlikely to be effective for, as interviews with members of HMI have highlighted, there is a clear need to debate issues of race equality and enable individuals to feel confident in using a common language and developing some shared understandings. The evidence we have gathered, both from HMI and from inspectors working in schools, suggests that for training to be effective, it will have to address issues of language and race equality more directly than the existing documentation on educational inclusion does. Not only is there a need for a common language through which race equality issues can be sensitively and confidently discussed, but race equality itself needs to be part of the corporate culture and everyday discourse of OFSTED and its leadership.

Glimpses into OFSTED culture

During the course of a group interview with three members of OFSTED, where two members of the senior management team were present, one senior manager told a story from his recent experience. This anecdote led to some joking among colleagues which, we believe, provides a glimpse of the working culture. This is the story, as told to the researcher. We have changed the name of the individual to whom it refers:

> My secretary, who is very dark-skinned and is African Caribbean, came back on Monday from four weeks in the West Indies. We greeted each other and I asked her how she was and she said, 'Oh, I am terribly sunburned' and she said it with a grin. And I thought she was joking and sort of 'Oh, come on Elaine!' you know. And she rolled up her sleeve on her arm and said: 'I *am* terribly sunburned!' [Laughter] You know, we do, I mean, I am conscious when I am talking about these issues, I am not always quite sure whether I am using the right sort of language when I talk.

At one level the story illustrates one person's ignorance that black people as well as white are likely to change colour when exposed to the sun. Perhaps more significantly, it was told with the express purpose of illustrating how difficult it can be to find the right language when talking about race. In particular, it was told to illustrate the potential for causing offence. As the story-teller, this member of the OFSTED senior management team went on to explain:

> The relationships, by and large, within the organisation [OFSTED] allow a broad approach to humour of that sort. Nobody takes any particular offence most of the time, but it is still something that white middle-aged males, you know, middle class males are quite conscious of, at least!

This remark led to some joking between the two members of the OFSTED senior management team:

HMI 1: We are the minority group actually ~ we are the oppressed!

HMI 2: Absolutely, yes!

HMI 1: It is time for equal opportunities as a male!

HMI 2: I'm going to start a bandwagon rolling.

Jokes and stories can be very revealing. We believe these highlight a need for greater awareness about race equality issues to be raised in OFSTED itself, as well as among contracted inspectors. As Sir Herman Ouseley, former Chair of the Commission for Racial Equality points out:

> Every institution or organisation in Britain has some inherent bias, which is reflected in its operational culture. That culture determines how things are done, who benefits, who suffers and who experiences discrimination and exclusion (Ouseley, 2000).

Every organisation also has dominant forms of discourse which may serve to include or exclude. Such jokes and stories serve to illustrate the urgency and importance of developing a corporate culture in which race equality is an explicit key principle, is confidently understood and is reflected in everyday decision-making and discourse.

Training for HMI

A question to members of HMI about the ways in which HMI develop their expertise on issues of race equality elicited the following response from a member of the senior management team:

> Well, of course the [school] inspection teams are not drawn from our firm of inspectors.

The implication was that since members of HMI are not engaged in the regular inspection of schools, such expertise is not critical. Another member of the senior management team explained how members of HMI can increase their understanding of race equality issues. It appears that there are two possible means: first, by taking advice from HMI team members who are specialists in the field; secondly, by participating in the preparation of guidance to inspectors and by reading that guidance. There was no example given of any formal training or any structured opportunities for groups of inspectors to discuss these issues:

> Yes, well, I mean, we have had a variety. I mean, we have ... Firstly we have HMI, who are specialists in each of these issues and very sort of finely-tuned specialists as well, whether it is behaviour, English as an additional language or whatever. ... So firstly, I think that there is quite a strong awareness and quite a long-standing culture of awareness of these issues within HMI, which is now a fairly small group of people of 200 or less. But we do, apart from frameworks and handbooks, we do periodically provide supplementary guidance for all inspectors, actually including HMI, drawn up by HMI, on things like the subjects of the curriculum and other important issues in schools, in which equal opportunities and special educational needs are two which [are] always included. And so

there is a wide input within the organisation into those documents, which we have for primary and for secondary schools, and a sort of wide involvement. There was consultation across all the appropriate divisions of OFSTED, the HMI working divisions, before they are published. And then they become almost supplements to the handbooks for inspectors in the field.

The member of HMI then went on to emphasise that OFSTED had training plans for all contracted inspectors following the publication of the Macpherson report:

> But, I mean, we have on the stocks, plans for a massive training programme in the light of Macpherson. You have new handbooks and changes to the national curriculum and so on over the next year or so, which will incorporate all inspectors, all the nine or ten thousand inspectors who are out there in the field. So we are doing substantial top-up training.

A problem with Macpherson?

Finally, a member of HMI questioned whether the definition of institutional racism put forward in the Macpherson report is helpful in the context of schooling and the inspection of schools. In particular, he questioned whether the Government response, which requires OFSTED to contribute to the prevention of racism through examining strategies in schools, is workable:

> I think there remains a problem which is a problem which will resolve itself in time. It is the application in the Home Office Plan to the definition of racism in the context of inspection and we know how that term – [we] can make it absolutely clear – how it can refer to events. But you see how the term 'racism' gets to be used. In that context [it is] unavoidable but it does require a lot more thinking, and sensitive thinking, to translate exactly that term in terms of school and inspection. And what inspection should focus on and what it can reveal about what it finds. There is absolutely no doubt in my mind that the things that you would need to look at in school in order to come to that view if you were asked exactly to report, exactly against the words of recommendation 69. All that you need to do is in there. And how you configure and organise the evidence to come to that view, that is a separate question. In a sense it lies outside the purpose of inspection.

It would appear that, one year after the Macpherson report was published, OFSTED has not arrived at a working definition of institutional racism which can be applied sensitively within the processes of school inspection. Nevertheless, it is argued that the current framework has all that is required to achieve such a defined understanding. There is, however, the suggestion that, even if a shared understanding of the meaning of institutional racism in education were agreed, the collection of evidence on the strategies schools are developing to counter and prevent racism in education lies outside the purposes of inspection.

Conclusion

We are led to understand that race equality will be a key feature of educational inclusion. The notion of 'educational inclusion' is to underpin training for contracted inspectors, although the timetable for this training has yet to be confirmed and it is not yet certain whether it will be mandatory. Evidence from our interviews suggests that race equality is not yet recognised as a central feature of educational inclusion by all at OFSTED. Currently race equality is seen by members of the OFSTED senior management team not as a key principle underpinning standards in education but as one of a number of 'baubles on the Christmas tree' of school inspection which, although important, may cause the tree to topple over.

Under the current inspection framework, there is still little guidance on monitoring by ethnicity. Members of HMI stress how the new framework encourages inspectors to evaluate a school's practices and identify differential achievement. There appears to be a conflation in the minds of some members of HMI, however, of the requirement to include ethnic composition among the characteristics of the school and the processes of monitoring by ethnicity. It is the processes of ethnic monitoring which would reveal any differentials between ethnic groups in attainment, in access to the school's services and provisions, and in the use of disciplinary procedures such as exclusion. There are also some uncertainties within HMI as to whether regular school inspection is capable of revealing evidence of racial harassment and bullying, although this is something that the Government requires OFSTED to monitor.

HMI recognises the need for 'a common language' when discussing issues of race equality. Yet some members of HMI, including some members of the OFSTED senior management team, themselves lack confidence in using such a language. Race equality has yet to become a central part of the corporate culture and discourse within OFSTED.

Chapter 4

INSPECTORS' PERSPECTIVES

At the cutting edge

I think that although [the goals of race equality] are implicit in there and I am sure it is the intention of a framework that looks at raising achievement and standards and attainment, it would be implicitly looking for race equality. You know, I believe that was the intention. I think in practice the framework wasn't clear enough about that and so that a school could do perfectly well without paying specific attention to race equality and could still come out quite well without paying any specific attention to race equality. The new one [framework] is moving in the right direction. I can still imagine that you can get a good report without necessarily having very explicit strategies in place. *Contracted inspector – EAL specialist.*

The inspection process itself is a fairly clumsy and unwieldy vehicle. The inspection framework does not really understand what the focuses of multicultural education and anti-racist education is all about. They are still tied into a historical view of multiculturalism ie if you teach children a lot of content, a lot of knowledge, content about diverse communities and other ways of life and cultures, then that will combat racism. There is very limited evidence of that, very limited evidence indeed, but the cultural dimension of the OFSTED framework is still locked into a historical time warp of 15-20 years ago. *LEA adviser*

Because you have an inspection system, whenever someone comes up with a new priority, they just dump it on the inspection system, and we have had this happen issue after issue, ever since we started, and sometimes at very short notice. We have not been briefed properly and the expectations have not been clear. As far as our teams are concerned, we have tried to address this [the Macpherson Report and its implications for inspection] corporately, by trying to tease out and debate among ourselves about these issues... Now I hope if someone from OFSTED overhears this then somebody says 'yes that is right, that is where we think it [inspection for race equality] ought to be' but I have no guarantee. If you want a detailed brief, you really have to stop and think about how you are going to equip your inspector to do this and carry it through, because it isn't just something that you can just give to people and say 'get on with it'. *Registered inspector*

These words preface this chapter dedicated to the perspectives of professionals who are required by Government to take a leading role in enabling schools to realise race equality through inspection. In-depth interview data came from six inspectors: in addition, supplementary interview data was obtained from a further three interviewees drawn from LEA advisers and headteachers who were also inspectors contracted to OFSTED. Each interview lasted at least sixty minutes, and all except one (at the interviewee's request) was tape-recorded and transcribed. In the following sections, analysis will focus upon the responses to questions addressed in the form of semi-structured interviews (see Appendix item 1).

Frameworks to support the goal of race equality

Framework 'prompts' and race equality

Most interviewees saw the previous framework (1996-1999) as providing a series of opportunities to collect and weigh up evidence that addressed broad equalities issues. They felt that the framework provided most of the necessary prompts to tease out equalities issues, including race equality, even if 'race equality has not been part of the language of inspection'. *The* key issue was the extent to which an inspection team had the capacity, skills, and knowledge to pull the relevant threads together to form a coherent holistic picture of a school's provision for equality. However, two inspectors argued that the framework did not support the goals of race equality; both considered the ways in which the OFSTED framework dealt with issues of equality to be too broad and thought that the end result was that it actually stultified attempts by LEA advisers to move schools on from a low level of awareness:

Myself and colleagues have experienced all sorts of concerns about a school that we would have picked up on, and certainly I can identify a whole range of schools where I think their provision in multiracial and anti-racist education is minimal. But the inspector has gone in and seen an assembly of Diwali and thought this is good... and have written credit-able things about the school, which has, to a certain extent, cut the ground from beneath the feet of people who are trying to move the school on. *LEA adviser and contracted inspector*

The role of reporting inspectors

The critical role of reporting inspectors was noted in all the interviews. In relation to equalities issues, their importance was seen to lie not only in their role as co-ordinators but, more importantly, in their instrumental steer towards supporting professional values in which issues of equality were prioritised. This was, it was considered, accomplished by some inspection team leaders but not all. Most interviewees could cite at least one example of inspection leadership having promoted coherent responses to equalities issues, but they also recognised both structural and professional obstacles to this happening.

No questions asked, no problems found

Whether an inspection team had awareness about race equality was considered to be a critical issue. Equally importantly, the structures that underpinned inspection could be used or ignored in various ways. If team members were unable to understand the prompts the framework provided *or* the significance of data collected in relation to equalities issues, they would not report on them. One inspector referred to this as a kind of 'colour-blindness' in which inspectors who lacked the conceptual capacity to address specific questions about equalities, made race equality a non-issue, either because they lacked awareness about equalities issues or because other issues were deemed more important. An interviewee considered this at length:

> If you go in as a blank slate you're not really looking because you're not really asking yourself [equalities] questions, and because you're not asking yourself those kinds of questions you are only open to receiving what you receive.

This interviewee went on to offer this example:

You could comment quite favourably about excellent parental involvement in school but if you unpick it, it is not reflective of the intake. When I did an inspection in [London] I went along with a registered inspector to the parents evening and it was interesting because it wasn't a big turn-out, mainly about forty parents. Now that school has a very diverse intake. The turnout was predominantly white – and predominantly, I would say middle class – with a sprinkling of parents from other minority groups. Now the middle class white parents were very supportive and articulate about the school. What I was conscious about was that several of the ethnic minority parents wanted to speak, I think another parent might have needed interpreting facilities made available. So what you could have received... what you could have taken as these parents had all spoken very positively about this school, was very positive messages....Actually, it was a worrying scenario for me ...because the turnout was too small for it to be a representative sample, and of the few minority parents who were there ...they looked and seemed very uncomfortable and were not supported when they spoke and their impact [was] marginalised.

Conflict avoidance

An inspector noted that issues could become dismissed if they were potentially unpleasant to report:

It is so often a kind of colour-blind inspector... It therefore needs obviously the registered inspector who is the person who is charged to make sure the process occurs according to the framework, and if you have got people on your team who are not looking with multi-coloured specs then you should make sure they are, so I think a lot of responsibility rests on the shoulders of the 'Regi'.

Concern was also shown that where the methods used to gather inspection evidence were insufficiently watertight, it would leave inspectors open to major conflict situations in a 'sensitive' area. Standardisation of response tended to by-pass difficult issues: for example, diluting references to specific groups, occasionally at the request of heads, as in the following example from an inspector:

I remember I had one head teacher saying to me 'Please don't use the word Travellers because I have so much backlash from my local parents about the way they are treated'. ... [The school] dealt with Travellers very effectively, but the head wanted me to pull out any reference to Travellers.

In response, this inspector took the decision to talk in more 'global terms' (his words) about 'the school's relationship with different sections of the community'.

A common framework for race equality?

Overall, then, the perspective was that the previous (1996-99) inspection framework had provided a common framework for reporting on race equality issues (and the current (2000) framework has the potential to promote more specific reporting) but the key issue was the extent to which the framework depends upon an inspection team, who, with appropriate leadership, share an awareness of the key elements of race equality. One interviewee considered that the interpretations of the framework by different inspection teams were sufficiently diverse to make the term 'common' redundant, and as importantly, to render any attempt at comparisons between schools highly problematic.

Ethnicity: pupil composition and school characteristics

Monitoring by ethnicity

The lack of specificity and consistency by schools in the way they reported the ethnic composition of the school population (issues also discussed in chapter five) received widespread comment. For inspectors, this was a matter of working with the data they were given; this data was often either incomplete or in multiple forms. Inspectors offered a range of interpretations and understandings about why this was so. Some blame was attached to schools for an insensitivity at school level about its own composition. There was also a tendency to view ethnic composition as an aspect of the 'context' in which inspectors were working rather than as a key issue for raising standards and attainment.

An experienced team inspector in the area of mathematics and equal opportunities stated that throughout his years of inspection, he had never come across attainment data by ethnicity, only by gender. The usual reason schools gave was 'lack of resources' to 'collect this kind of data'. The inspector considered that this was a rather 'strange rationale', given that schools collected 'tons of data' that related to issues other than ethnic minority achievement.

A training need

Other inspectors thought schools required training in the collection and analysis of accurate and appropriate data for monitoring and evaluating the progress of pupils by ethnicity. In an authority where an interviewee had worked, schools had been given LEA data on attainment by 'ethnic breakdown in GCSEs', which 'the authority had done for years', but 'schools don't make a good deal of use of that data, I would say, even though they have data on outcomes, they're not used to saying 'well what does this tell us and what does this mean for our practice?'' The role of the LEA in collecting appropriate data was considered critical, as this had an impact on the quality of data collected at school level. The accuracy of the data also impacted on the quality of questions the inspection team were able to ask, a point which links back to earlier comments about inspectors' awareness equipping them to ask the key questions.

It was not just schools who needed guidance on ethnic monitoring. Evidence from one inspector suggested that he did not understand its value. This inspector was sympathetic to those schools who were ill at ease with ethnic monitoring and he saw it as a process whereby an identity was imposed on each individual, rather than one in which self-identification is a key factor.

> We find it very difficult to identify youngsters according to any sort of list. It goes back to my earlier point about families that describe themselves as Black British, why should they be seen as different? I know that some schools have difficulties in terms of establishing from parents and the youngster what categories they fit in. You know, the whole thing is a difficulty. I think it is more a difficulty than an excuse.

The following comment from a member of HMI seems to sum up the range of approaches inspectors use for describing the pupil populations whose educational standards and quality of education they are inspecting:

> I guess there are schools that won't have very good descriptions of their populations, that won't have broken down certain categories like 'Asian'

or whatever, because I assume that where certain inspection reports are using unhelpful categories... they have been given that information in that form, unless they've chosen to group it in that form... It's difficult to tell whether the inspectors are simply rehashing what they've got from the school and its governing body, or whether they are putting a gloss on the information. It's difficult to know when you read a report cold, it's difficult to know where they're getting that.

Monitoring and evaluating educational standards

Interviewees were much clearer about the shortcomings in schools' monitoring and evaluation procedures of pupils' progress by ethnicity than they were about the extent to which their own strategies – like classroom observation, teacher interviews, and document analysis – were able to overcome the very serious deficiency in effective monitoring. Inspectors pointed out that schools' documented evidence about key stage and examination attainments often failed to identify the needs of specific groups 'in any sophisticated way'. Attainment for pupils with special educational needs, because it was a specifically focused area of school interest, was often 'easier' to collect and analyse than the patterns of attainment and achievement by ethnicity.

Invisibility of different groups

Interviewees also commented that the lack of accurate monitoring had a further effect in homogenising 'black and ethnic minority groups' as if their needs were all alike. This meant not only that the needs of specific groups remained hidden but also that the limited data available either under-emphasised or exaggerated aspects of pupils' attainment, achievements, progress and needs.

Curriculum issues

In general terms, inspectors discussed the curriculum almost as if it were a kind of educational 'diet' in which they needed to show sensitivity both to the presence of ethnic minority pupils in the school and to pupils' cultural development (see below). They acknowledged that reporting on the curriculum varied, with some reports containing more illustrative examples from specific subject areas than others. Several interviewees were conscious of schools' reluctance for inspection reports to draw upon specific examples of practice, 'not so much when it's positive, but they're very much opposed when it isn't'.

Several inspectors commented on a range of evidence that might be drawn from material on display, examples taken from classroom observations and from school documents supplied before the inspection. It was considered that evidence of whole school approaches was less commonly available; one interviewee explained that 'pieces of evidence' were passed around for discussion within the team, then 'weighed up and balanced' during the inspection week, and the role of the reporting inspector was 'absolutely critical' in determining whether such evidence was actually included in the report.

Among the conclusions we draw is that inspectors feel that evidence of good practice within curriculum areas tends to be under-emphasised, with reports focusing more commonly on whole school developments. It appears that inspectors are more comfortable with making judgements about 'whole school approaches'. Even if these comments are somewhat superficial, they prefer generalised rather than specific examples of good practice. Moreover, as an inspector noted 'you would want to know if such [curriculum] materials were routinely used, and it's very difficult to ascertain that'.

Provision for pupils with English as an additional language

The importance of this area was stressed by inspectors but they recognised that expertise to deliver incisive judgements in EAL had been limited, 'particularly in the early days', by the scarcity of expertise. The records kept by schools about pupils with EAL were less rigorous, it was considered, than those kept for pupils with SEN. A primary school inspector who was also an EAL specialist commented:

> The composition of OFSTED teams have always been put together, you know, to cover the core curriculum areas. But you could have an English specialist that didn't have any EAL background, there would be no need why they would do, you know in terms of teams across the whole country. And another couple of worrying instances I had once before in [my previous LEA] was where an inspector... found he was going to do an inspection in a [London borough] school and came to see me to see if he could find out something about Section 11 before he went.

76

Several examples of effective practice in the area were noted, such as the following in which an inspector describes:

> One school with a high level of mobility, so they get lots of refugees in as well as other mobile pupils who are not refugees, so the EAL issue is a big issue for the school, but it's not the only issue. The school is working on lots of fronts. With the EAL they have got funded through EMAG, they have got a new arrivals teacher whose job it is to induct new pupils and work with parents and look at some of the teaching and learning programmes for the pupils that come in. ...It is done well and it is a very supportive environment and the result in terms of attainment in that school is that they do very well in science and quite well in maths and less so in English...That headteacher plots all her children on a kind of matrix and she has SEN on one grid and EAL on another as they move round the school. And the level of support is kind of overlaid, she has a very carefully thought out model of what each child gets and what kinds of support... they are targeting carefully in terms of needs, so for EAL pupils, that works well.

The quality of reporting on the teaching of EAL in schools where there were few such pupils was of equal, if not more interest to inspectors. It was recognised that if inspectors made judgements that were more generally focused upon English and/or literacy overall, then specific language needs might be overlooked, or more commonly subsumed, as part of more general interests in the attainment and progress of all pupils. No interviewees offered detailed rationales on their approaches to pupil withdrawal or in-class support.

Inspecting white schools

Inspectors were invited to consider the specific features they would look for in predominately white schools which would demonstrate that the school is addressing racism and promoting race equality. This was an issue that focused the minds of all interviewees, one of whom presented an interesting view of a differentiated society in which white youngsters would need to cross geographical as well as career boundaries at some time in the future, so that:

> Inspectors should go in with the same range of questions but that some questions are more important than others. All white schools would be characteristic of a number of comprehensives in [this LEA] and again we

have been keen that youngsters address the issue of racial equality. Of course, many go on to higher education and go to cities and find themselves in a multicultural society. So it is relevant to them...You can imagine a school saying 'well it doesn't matter we haven't got any of those' – we would challenge that very strongly.

Several interviewees suggested that the issue of race equality was 'more important' in white or predominantly white schools. This viewpoint is not reflected in the inspection reports, where the evidence of reporting on race equality in predominantly white schools is sparse (see chapter five). A refreshing perspective came from one interviewee, who was the only person to identify multi-ethnic schools as a cause of celebration rather than a problem:

It's obviously as important or more important for all-white schools to prepare pupils to promote equality and to promote awareness of pupils, an awareness that they may not have around and about them the same way as [London] pupils will have. You know [London] pupils are privileged to live in this sort of society because they meet pupils from different kind of backgrounds all the time and if [some] white pupils don't do that then those schools have to work harder. [A white school] should work harder at promoting awareness and so I think that the way to do it would be to put more specific guidance into the OFSTED framework around what [such] schools are expected to do.

One of the challenges of inspection, we were informed, was getting 'beneath the surface' of what appeared to be good race equality indicators in schools. Even where white or predominantly white schools 'have been kick-started' into action when they received judgements about the need for 'more cultural awareness', they were often unclear about how to improve their practice. A senior LEA officer considered that insufficient pointers were given to schools by inspection teams about what the term meant and what schools should do about it.

Pupils' spiritual, moral, social and cultural development

Inspectors were agreed on three issues: *first*, that this was the section of the report where many of the aspects that related to 'cultural diversity' and 'equalities issues' were centred; *second*, that this was also the arena in which the collection and analysis of evidence was most challenging; and that *third*, its concentration into this area tended to reinforce a view that ethnic minority pupils are seen as presenting attitudinal or social problems or challenges to schools. This distracts attention from two key issues: the need to ensure high standards for all pupils regardless of ethnicity, and the need for schools themselves to make structural changes to ensure equality of access to everything the school has to offer.

Another concern expressed by inspectors was the tendency for giving responsibility for the collection of data of this kind to a lay inspector. One interviewee commented on this in these rather disparaging terms:

> I think there is some potential in identifying that schools are not dealing effectively with the needs of black students, but the quality of inspection [of spiritual, moral, social and cultural development] is extraordinarily varied. And you might get one who actually understands what the issues relating to cultural diversity or the issues relating to black achievement actually are. You might get another team who look at SMSC who really haven't got a clue. It's given to the lay inspector or somebody who happens to have a subject specialism in RE because it seems to fit into that, which is a very restricted view of what spiritual, moral, social, and cultural development is all about ... I don't think the framework is at all anywhere near the cutting edge.

An inspector queried the grouping of the categories – spiritual, moral, social and cultural development of pupils – together, arguing that the tendency was to downplay or ignore specific criticisms in one area if the other three were judged to be meeting pupils' needs satisfactorily or better.

Racial harassment and bullying

There was a general acknowledgement that collecting evidence specifically about racial harassment or bullying was very challenging. A most disturbing account was given by an inspector who had himself experienced racial taunts and harassment in classrooms and corridors during the inspection. Yet the team had been willing to comment positively in the inspection report about the effectiveness of the school's procedures for combating racial bullying and harassment.

The starting point for one interviewee was the need for an acceptance by contracted inspectors that 'racism exists'; the challenge was to try and 'dig' beneath the surface of, for example, bullying incident books that did not always specify whether the context of the incident *was* racial. Moreover, several interviewees pondered the credibility of evidence collected from small groups of school-selected pupils. Sensitivity and care were seen to be key issues:

> The big issue is whether inspection teams actually understand what institutionalised racism is and how that can be demonstrated through the school curriculum, through a school's ethos, through the school's prospectus, through the school's display, and through the things a school celebrates and the things that a school ignores... I am not sure that the average OFSTED inspector who goes in with an SMSC hat on, with a range of other aspect responsibilities, could do that.

This perspective was reinforced by an HMI who noted that:

> Nearly all youngsters, like minority ethnic youngsters, suffer some form of racial harassment, discrimination, almost on a daily basis, whether it is on the way to school, whether it is at school, through gesture, it might be other pupils, it might be remarks from teachers, or whatever.

Much 'digging' was therefore required to ascertain whether race equality was 'fine' in a school. A need was also seen for moving beyond a position of identifying 'racial tension' as a phenomenon that existed between black and white students in a school to also recognising racist attitudes that might be 'held by kids in all-white schools'.

School leadership

The role of the head teacher in race equality matters was considered crucial. Inspectors recognised that most attention was given to the way in which effective management was maximised in terms of the best and most efficient use of resources to effect school improvement and quality of education for all pupils. One interviewee linked her comments to the area of spiritual development:

> The extent to which spirituality is promoted varies according to the headteacher I think. That is my experience from here. But you can still have headteachers who promote a respect for all the other religions without there necessarily being a spiritual dimension to any of them and I think that is what we should be looking at. In terms of race equality you would be looking for faith equality as well... Not the religions done

for their kind of exotic aspects, you do see that don't you... Now I think that church schools struggle with that, but you still can, you know, if it's handled sensibly by the head.

Staffing

Inspectors cited examples of the importance of giving support to specialist staff who had specific responsibilities for ethnic minority students, in order that these and all staff felt confident that such interests were not being marginalised. One interviewee explained how he looked at staff job descriptions and made sure that senior management teams were looking at equal opportunities from the reference points of race and gender. This area of inspection often focused on documents – usually policy documents produced by the head and senior management team (SMT). There was less evidence from the interview data that inspection teams examined not only the staffing profile (for its degree of match with the pupil profile) but also the ethnic composition of governing bodies. Inspectors' comments were supported by our analysis of school inspection reports (chapter five) where comments on such issues are rare. One inspector observed that 'race equality issues ought to be evident in staff appraisal issues and staff review, but they rarely are'.

Inspectors drew further evidence about the role of the head and the SMT from the way relationships with parents and the community were developed; this required an active commitment that is pursued by the headteacher. One interviewee believed schools sometimes digressed from key issues: ' in this area [geographical location] more schools are striving for the *Investors in People* award. The real question is, investors in which people?' The implication here is that schemes such as *Investors in People* have not, until very seriously, begun to require participants to ensure race equality. The real value of the award is thus undermined.

Relationships with parents and the community

Perspectives on the relationship between schools and parents and the community have featured in earlier sections. An interesting point made by two interviewees related to the extent to which the framework played sufficient attention to multi-agency collaboration. As one pointed out:

> There are some really interesting initiatives going on and you know the relationship between LEAs and schools is quite different from how it used to be. I mean we are not the only ones to be working with schools, we are not expected to be the only provider of race equality initiatives... it would be nice if the OFSTED framework could pull out these things. I think that they rarely do.

Headteachers were considered to play a key role in promoting multi-agency collaboration, a role which, it was considered, was not always visible:

> What I think doesn't come through is when heads are particularly good at promoting race equality. It's seen as a bit of a sideline.

Promoting race equality internally and in the wider community was felt to be an issue that came through in some reports more than others. An inspector who was also an adviser noted that in her authority:

> We have got some really good schools in [this LEA] that really do promote race equality, where you feel the head is leading a strong ethos, but I have hardly ever picked up...We have probably trawled through the reports and hardly ever seen that when I have read a report. It might be down under 'cultural', I suppose.

Failing schools

Interviewees noted a number of factors, which might cause a school to be labelled a failing school. One interviewee called this 'a four-pronged approach', the prongs being: the educational standards achieved by the school; the quality of education provided; whether the financial resources of the school were appropriately and efficiently managed; and the spiritual, moral, social and cultural development of pupils. While the 'quality of pupil relationships' was embedded within these 'prongs' and might or might not include evidence of racial harassment or bullying, it was felt that prominent weighting was 'invariably' given to issues of standards and attainment. One interviewee was adamant that issues of race inequality had never featured strongly in any of the inspections he had been involved with in relation to failing schools.

Another perspective was that even in schools that were judged to be in need of special measures, insufficient attention was, on occasion, paid to the positive efforts being made in relation to race equality. For example, an inspector pointed out that 'in a school that went into special measures' where 'lots of things were wrong', 'the one thing that was really working well' was the EMAG team, and 'the only thing that was pulled out was that 'the school responds well to pupils' cultural needs".

Ways forward

Interviewees were unanimous about the potential of the previous OFSTED framework to promote the goal of race equality in schools. Nevertheless they felt that the potential of the former and current framework was likely to be undermined by inadequate resources. In particular they identified the need for resources to address the training needs of both schools and inspectors.

Interviewees argued that since 'OFSTED drives so much of what schools do', OFSTED was in a pivotal position to promote race equality. What was required was a level of specificity that neither framework had so far achieved. Training for inspectors and for schools was considered essential:

> Something needs to be attached to the framework for race equality whereby specific things are looked at and that inspectors could learn how to do it. It would be a start, if they said that no-one could be an inspector unless you did the 'equalities' training, the literacy training, the numeracy training...

There was also widespread scepticism among the inspectors concerning OFSTED's level of commitment to race equality. One interviewee was vehement in his view that any action plan to promote race equality that involved inspectors would be both a 'waste of time' and 'an act of sheer hypocrisy' if no resources were provided, and that such a misguided approach was underpinned by a mistaken view that inspectors alone 'could sort things out'. The general view was that, for OFSTED, race equality was just one of many obligations but one that was not being given high status or priority.

One interviewee was concerned that if, as a result of this research, more emphasis was placed on race equality and inclusion, he would be ill-prepared to carry out his role. Government's interest in social inclusion and Citizenship education was welcomed only if it was to be accompanied by a transparent OFSTED model and serious commitment to addressing issues of race equality.

If the developmental role fell to LEAs, then several interviewees sought more 'joined up thinking' about the respective contributions of OFSTED and LEAs. The majority view, however, was that if race equality was not going to be rigorously inspected, and if the message came through to schools that this was not an area of key concern either to OFSTED or to the Government, then schools 'who might not be inclined to carry on work like that' would continue to operate as before.

A message to the top

The final words of this chapter go to an LEA adviser who had worked in both inner city and rural schools. He expressed what he believed HMCI should be saying on the subject of racial justice in education in order for OFSTED to make a real contribution to addressing and preventing racism in schools:

> Emphasising that every school has a fundamental responsibility for preparing children for the sort of society they are going to live in, which would mean things like dealing with the particular learning needs very sympathetically of all children, irrespective of what their cultural origins were. Focusing in the minds of schools that they really need to get a grip on oppressive behaviour and it's more than just bullying in the playground, and that work on racism really needs to equip children with the skills that they will need to challenge inappropriate attitudes as they grow older. That ought to be done with increasing levels of sophistication, starting with pre-school and continuing in a coherent way right through to the end of state education.

> It will mean children knowing and empathising with and celebrating different groups of people and their backgrounds that they are going to be working with on a day to day basis as they grow up. Because even in the wilds of []-shire children are not going to be growing up and working there, they are going to be working in all kinds of diverse contexts and they are going to need the skills and knowledge to operate in that.

> So the multicultural bit is important, but it needs to be alongside a rigorous anti-racist analysis of society and equipping children to handle

it. So that's what I'd like to hear a Chief Inspector say, and say that all inspection teams do need to have a central focus on this. And that the cultural dimension is all well and good, children do need cultural know - ledge, but what they actually need more than this is the skills to be able to challenge and combat racism.

Chapter 5

SCHOOL INSPECTION REPORTS

Inspecting the 'inspectable'?

Racial equality is not ...a teaching programme because it is a set of behaviours and characteristics, and therefore *less inspectable* I suppose. *Senior OFSTED official* (our emphasis)

In previous chapters, we examined the OFSTED inspection framework in its previous 1996-99 form (OFSTED, 1995) and new form from January 2000 (OFSTED, 1999d). We conclude that although both have the potential to make a key contribution to OFSTED's lead responsibility to prevent racism in schools, current efforts are likely to be hampered as long as OFSTED and its leadership continue to avoid detailed explicit discussion of race equality in its policy documents and public statements.

In this chapter, we draw upon illustrative evidence from a selection of *Section 10* reports compiled between 1997 and 1999. Analysis is framed in response to a series of questions (see below) that were developed from our summary of provision to inspect race equality in the 1996-99 framework (table 2.1). We will demonstrate that while race equality is 'inspectable', the effectiveness of such inspection has, to date, been undermined by:

invisibility of race equality as an inspection 'term', and by the dilution of equalities issues in inspection

inconsistency in the frequency and quality of reporting race equality issues

marginality of race equality issues and disparate monitoring and evaluation strategies

over-reliance upon a language of generalised and limited 'equalities' statements

inadequacy of attention to race equality issues in predominantly white schools

limited expertise in the reporting of English as an additional language (EAL).

The literature review

Our intensive analysis of report documents was underpinned by a literature review that afforded general insight into OFSTED inspections. There is, however, limited literature on the specific issue of inspecting for race equality. The summary below provides a brief synthesis of research as it relates to inspection overall and, where available, to race equality.

Support for rigorous quality management

Published research on OFSTED inspections is plentiful and provides overall support for the rigorous quality management of all the services schools provide. Positive accounts of inspection in practice suggest that inspection has:

- encouraged schools to identify or acknowledge specific weaknesses in their policies and practices, and to address these through their action plans (Wilcox and Gray, 1995)

- identified schools that are doing well, and highlighted such schools as examples of good practice

- acted as a focus for schools to prepare for inspection, thereby facilitating some forms of self-evaluation (Ponchaud, 1997)

- ensured that the work of inspection teams is regarded as professional, pertinent to the school and supportive of school development (CEPPP, 1999; Maychell and Pathak, 1997).

Criticisms

In less positive accounts, critics argue that inspection:

- combines, and therefore confuses, the separate tasks of a quality management system, namely quality as being – assurance; control; audit; assessment; and enhancement (Doherty, 1994)

- depends on a centralised and inadequate notion of educational quality

- separates the processes of inspection and the provision of support for improvement, and treats schools as static rather than dynamic organisations (Hopkins, *et al*, 1999)

- lacks process measures (MacBeath, 1999)

- raises doubts about the reliability and validity of inspections (Fidler, Earley and Ouston, 1996; Fitz-Gibbon and Stephenson-Forster, 1999)

- raises concerns that inspectors do not always have adequate expertise in the subjects/aspects they are observing (Millett and Johnson, 1998).

Race equality, inspection and fitness for purpose

Our resumé of published findings suggests that if inspection frameworks are to contribute to the promotion of race equality, they should be expected to meet most, and preferably all, of the following objectives to:

- exemplify a general professional willingness to be accountable to all local communities and to the public at large (CEPPP, 1999)

- build on the willingness of teachers and schools to be inspected by suitable outsiders (Maychell and Pathak, 1997)

- produce accounts of schools based on what actually happens in them, rather than relying on guesswork or single measures of educational output

- be rigorous and treat all schools equally

- provide feedback which can inform policy and practice at a number of levels (Fidler and Ouston, 1996)

- draw upon objective, moderated and professional judgements as the basis of the report (Ouston, Earley and Fidler, 1996).

See also Watling (2000) for review of the literature on inspection and fitness for purpose.

Our literature review provided pointers about the extent to which the analysis of inspection reports should:

- provide an accurate picture of the health of the nation's schools system in promoting race equality, as well as detailed accounts of individual schools

- employ standardised procedures to improve the comparability of reports, and

- produce frameworks that are open to revision.

Inspection and race equality

To date, however, there has been a paucity of published work on inspection and race equality issues. This is in marked contrast to research that has highlighted how seriously schools fail to meet the needs of pupils from black and ethnic minority communities (Gillborn and Gipps, 1996), racial inequalities in the use of school exclusions (Osler and Hill, 1999), racial harassment in schools (Home Office, 1996), and teachers' expectations of black and ethnic minority pupils (Wright, 1992a, 1992b).

An exception is Richardson's (1994) research into the first fifty inspection reports, where the author concludes that the attention given to equality of opportunities could lead parents and governors to assume that equal opportunity issues were of only 'very slight importance' in judgements about the overall effectiveness of schools (1994: 4). Equalities issues were mentioned in only twenty per cent of the 'main findings' sections of these fifty initial reports, and no report identified behaviour and discipline as equal opportunities concerns, even in schools where ethnic minority pupils were being disproportionately excluded.

The report *Raising the Attainment of Minority Ethnic Pupils* (OFSTED 1999g) was part of OFSTED's response to DfEE concerns about the achievement of ethnic minority pupils as evidenced, for example, in Gillborn and Gipp's review (1996), and also to problems of racial tension and harassment in schools, identified by the inter-departmental Racial Attacks Group (Home Office, 1996). However, the focus of this report was upon key monitoring and management issues for schools and LEAs, rather than upon the contribution of OFSTED inspection through its processes and practices.

This external rather than introspective focus is continued in OFSTED reports examining schools' effectiveness in monitoring and reducing exclusions (OFSTED, 1996, 1999g). A survey of 48 schools revealed a failure to monitor or comprehensively analyse pupil behaviour by ethnicity. It concluded that 'this leaves schools open to the danger of stereotypical 'impressions' and gives no sound basis for initiatives to address any real difficulties' (OFSTED 1999g: para.121).

Our approach to document analysis

In *Section 10* reports, inspectors must by law report on: the educational standards achieved by the school; the quality of education provided; whether the financial resources made available to the school are managed efficiently; and the spiritual, moral, social and cultural development of pupils. Our approach to document analysis was in the context of an inspection framework that includes a range of documents to inform and guide inspection teams. These include:

- forms completed by the school before the inspection

- the previous inspection report and action plan

- Pre-inspection Context and School Indicator (PICSI) data

- parents' views as expressed in the pre-inspection meeting and the parents' questionnaire

- the headteacher's report

- guidance on inspecting for Equal Opportunities (EO) and English as an additional language (EAL) (OFSTED, 1999e,1999f).

Document analysis involved several stages, as outlined here in chapter one.

We asked: What questions need to be posed about an inspection framework to determine whether issues of equality and social justice are integral? (Our response is shown as Appendix item 4.) Key phrases, sentences and sections were copied and highlighted from the final reports and examples of unpublished data, and these were linked to the questions. This allowed for examination of reports as written accounts that had passed through stages of construction, categorisation and standardisation.

OFSTED documents

A final inspection report is the end product of procedures that draw upon primary and secondary sources and from evidence from quantitative and qualitative investigative strategies. Consequently, we studied a range of OFSTED documents that inform school inspections.

Standardisation

All documents for inspection are collected and analysed in accordance with the prescribed OFSTED procedures. Whereas the current framework emphasises that 'the content and wording must not follow any pre-determined structure' (OFSTED, 1999d:8), the prescribed format for all previous reports has, in effect, produced outcomes that are expressed in very similar terms, and the judgements about each school included standardised and graded expressions. Some assessments of schools' performances are compared with national standards and with standards in 'similar' schools. The reports made only limited reference to the terms 'race equality' or 'racial equality'. Although equalities 'prompts' were generally embedded in the framework, our hypothesis that they were insufficiently explicit to demand more than minimal attention in the final reports was largely confirmed. Many race and other equality issues became 'invisible' and, as this chapter shows, did nothing to challenge the view that 'no mention' meant 'no problem'.

Matching inspection teams and schools

Before inspections took place, schools completed forms (now known as S1, S2, S3 and S4, OFSTED, 1999h) to provide information for OFSTED to send to the inspection contractor. On the basis of this knowledge the inspection contractor brings together an inspection team that 'match [es] the circumstances and curriculum of the school' (S1).

We explored several interpretations of the term 'matching' and considered their implications for our study:

Matching expertise to pupils' needs

Initial scanning of the reports indicated wide variations in schools' data on the ethnic composition of the pupil population and pupils with English as an additional language. So, for example, whether or not an inspection team included an inspector with EAL responsibility would have depended partly on the accuracy of the pupil composition data provided. This has implications for the appropriateness of the match between the inspection team and the character and circumstances of the school.

Matching inspection team characteristics to school characteristics

If the term 'matching' is understood to include a similarity between the ethnic profile of the inspection team and the ethnic composition of the pupil population, there appears to be a major challenge in selecting team members for specific schools. Figure 5.1 shows the ethnic composition of registered and lay inspectors contracted to OFSTED, as provided by OFSTED. Although the data supplied to us by OFSTED is divided into two categories, 'white' and 'others' (and not all forms are completed), it can be seen that black and ethnic minority inspectors are under-represented among contracted inspectors. For comparative purposes we include in Figure 5.2 the ethnic composition of HMI. Here too there is a gross under-representation of black and ethnic minority employees.

Matching multiple responsibilities

In an analysis of 17 reports (only 17 of our original sample of 30 gave information about inspection teams on the OFSTED web-site), we noted the tendency to allocate aspects of pupils' personal development, pupils' guidance and support, and relations with parents and the community to the lay inspector (where identified). Key equalities

FIGURE 5.1: Ethnic breakdown of contracted inspectors

	NUMBER	PERCENTAGE
REGISTERED INSPECTORS	1898	100
Ethnic classification data		
Form not completed	41	2
White	1818	96
Others	39	2
LAY INSPECTORS	700	100
Ethnic classification data		
Form not completed	37	5
White	626	90
Others	37	5
TEAM INSPECTORS (INCLUDING RGIs)	2043	100
Ethnic classification data		
Form not completed	53	2
White	1931	95
Others	59	3
REGISTED NURSERY INSPECTORS	2043	100
Ethnic classification data		
Form not completed	53	2
White	1931	95
Others	59	3

(Data supplied by Research Department, OFSTED, 1999)

FIGURE 5.2: Ethnic breakdown of HMI

The ethnic breakdown of HMI is as follows:

White	95.3%
Black Caribbean	1.6%
Black African	0.5%
Asian/Indian	1%
Unknown	1.6%

(figures and format supplied by Research Department, OFSTED, 1999) issues were interpreted as the responsibility to examine 'what is generally known to be important in all schools' rather than as a focus for specific expertise and knowledge. As we have highlighted in chapter two, the current and previous frameworks do not require *expertise* in equal opportunities (EO) or EAL, only that an individual takes *responsibility* for these aspects of inspection.

Team members who had inspection responsibilities for EO or EAL were found to have multiple responsibilities in the team. For example, among inspectors with responsibilities for EO, seven carried between four and six additional responsibilities each. Of the two inspectors with EAL responsibilities, one carried six and the other two additional responsibilities. There appeared to be no consistent pattern in attaching EO to inspectors with particular subject or aspect responsibilities or to specific kinds of inspectors, although those carrying EAL responsibilities also had English as a subject responsibility.

In brief, data analysis from a sample sub-set illustrates a tendency to allocate EO responsibilities to inspectors carrying at least two other responsibilities. The tendency for carrying multiple responsibilities increases in certain schools, for example, smaller primary schools. The evidence suggests that, in an inspection arena where procedural specificity is key, consistency in the relation between EO and other inspection team responsibilities was seldom apparent and this is reinforced by a focus upon subject specific rather than EO expertise in contractual agreements.

Statistical data from schools

Statistical data from schools formed a key element of the evidence base for inspection between 1997 and 1999, and included attainment data by key stage, by examinations and by gender – but not by ethnicity. Reports included attendance and exclusions data, but this information is not consistently recorded by gender and ethnicity. We noted in chapter two that requirements for statistical data have been made more specific since 2000.

Initial scanning of the statistical data in the reports alerted us to several issues:

- the limitations of the schools in supplying data on attainment, exclusions and attendance by ethnicity

- inconsistencies in the expression of contextual data related to school characteristics and the ethnic composition of the pupil population

- variations in the proficiency of schools in distinguishing between pupils with EAL and pupils with SEN, and between pupils at different stages of English language acquisition, together with concerns about the capacity of the framework and the expertise of the inspection teams to disentangle these (see also below).

- inconsistency in the judgements about what constituted 'high' or 'low' levels of exclusions; variations in classifications by gender and by ethnicity, and lack of information about schools' reintegration policies and practices following exclusion.

Inspection team documents

Documents are central to the work of inspectors, informing both formative and summative judgements. The lead inspector prepares a pre-inspection analysis based upon: initial visits to the school; an analysis of the previous inspection report; headteacher forms; the PICSI report; and other documents like the prospectus and School Development Plan. S/he will, in addition, have data from the pre-inspection parents' meeting and the parents' questionnaire. Again, we identified a number of issues relating to our research.

Data from parents

Standardised documents are used for the pre-inspection meeting with parents and the minutes of that meeting are incorporated into the inspector's pre-inspection commentary. Data from the parents' questionnaire forms part of the final published report.

We noted that:

- the availability of interpreters at the parents' meeting was at the discretion of the governing body rather than being prescribed by inspectors

- there was no reference to equalities issues either in questionnaires to parents or in the standardised agenda for the parents' meeting

- there were variations in approach to the commentaries linked to the questionnaires, in particular the detail with which issues raised by individual parents were considered in the main report.

PICSI data

'Inspectors must provide a concise, factual statement about the characteristics of the school and its pupils and area it serves'. PICSI data from OFSTED provides the lead inspector with 'broad proxy indicators' about a school's characteristics, where possible in relation to national averages, and in relation to similar schools. Comparative attainment levels are calculated on the basis of combined OFSTED and DfEE figures on the number of pupils eligible for free school meals, divided by the number of pupils of compulsory school age on roll. Contextual data also informs the inspection process as it relates to: attainment and progress; attitudes; behaviour and personal development; the management and efficiency of the school; previous inspection grades; and statistical data about pupils on roll, pupils with SEN, gender, and pupils eligible for free school meals.

On the reporting of equalities issues, we noted several issues:

Local comparisons

While inspection teams are encouraged to make comparisons with local indicators from the LEA, initial report scanning suggested *first* that this was not being applied consistently across inspection reports, and, *second*, as OFSTED notes, that the progress pupils make in some LEAs might be neither representative of the national picture nor representative of LEAs with similar pupil populations. There was potential for the attainment of specific groups to be under or over-emphasised in relation to local circumstances.

Ethnicity and EAL

There was also some confusion in the way contextual information was given about ethnicity and EAL. In the PICSI Annex for primary schools (OFSTED, 1999i), for example, the two were considered together under the heading 'Ethnic Groups and English as an Additional Language'. Such combination is curious in an inspection framework which recognises each category as distinct if at times overlapping.

National averages were not given for pupils with EAL on grounds that 'the concentration of pupils in certain areas would make the national average misrepresentative'. The advice to ignore national averages in relation to pupils with EAL was not followed in several reports, in which we found that proportions of such pupils were recorded as 'less' or 'more than' the national average.

It is interesting to note that the degree of caution advocated in the use of 'national averages' as it related to EAL is not evident in all the statements contained in the Annex. In this document that purports to offer appropriate support data for inspection teams, the following statement is very misleading:

> Pupils' attainment in schools with high ethnic minority populations tends to be lower than in schools with small ethnic minority populations. This, however, can largely be explained by the socio-economic characteristics of ethnic minority populations. (PICSI annex 1, OFSTED, 1999i)

The statement does not make clear whether this refers to all pupils or those from ethnic minorities.

Socio-economic circumstances and the ethnicity 'problem'

Clearly, ethnic diversity was identified in reports as an issue of potential disadvantage rather than cause for celebration. 'The percentage of ethnic minority children' was supplied as one source of background information about the disadvantaged socio-economic circumstances in the wards surrounding the school. Ethnic minority pupils are problematised in the PICSI annex in relation to both contextual and attainment data. This is in notable contrast to the relative absence of any 'problem' in inspection reports, typified in phrases like '*there are no differences in attainment between ethnic groups*' (for detailed analysis see below). The frequent use of this and similar phrases had certainly occupied at least one HMI, who in interview said this about reports written under the 1996-99 framework:

The phrase is burned in my mind because I've read it that often, 'There are no differences in attainment between ethnic groups'. ... If it is true, then it is a remarkable institution because it, at the individual level, it is acting against all the trends that appear from the national data. ...One was kind of left with a second question. 'Is there any other evidence from the report that this school has really tackled race equality in a consistent way?' ...And the trouble is, it [the evidence] wasn't often there. *Member of HMI* (our emphasis)

From pre-inspection commentary to inspection week: the transformation of documented evidence

The collection of documents is a critical aspect of the pre-inspection analysis. Document analysis is at the front of the notebooks for inspection and it forms the basis upon which the inspection team formulates initial hypotheses. As evidence, it is triangulated with the data collected and coded during inspection week. This is then categorised in formats that apply standardised codes, culminating in a record of summative judgements called the Judgement Recording Form (Appendix item 5). We wished to understand the extent to which equalities issues identified in the pre-inspection analysis were developed/retained during and by the process of inspection.

In the following example (Figure 5.3), we illustrate some of the ways in which such issues were re-framed and transformed during inspection. Our commentary on pre-inspection and final report data appears in italics. The text in inverted commas is report text. The remaining text is made up of summarised extracts from the final report. In particular, we note how interest in attainment by ethnicity, behavioural issues, and the problems posed by specific groups were transformed into final overall judgements of 'good'. The only 'weak' areas in the final record are that the school 'does not *significantly* monitor the quality of its provision' and that '*significant* numbers of pupils are late to school each day' (our emphasis). In brief, the figure illustrates how pre-inspection data and inspectors' questions are transformed into the final report. In the process, certain issues relating to ethnicity are lost.

FIGURE 5.3. How a final report emerges from pre-inspection evidence

THE STRENGTHS OUTWEIGH THE WEAKNESS BUT...
Trieshard Primary School

Trieshard Primary School is located in a London Borough. The school has a pupil population of 252 pupils and is located in an area of mixed housing and socio-economic deprivation. School characteristics include the following: 'there is a higher than average number of pupils for whom English is an additional language. There are 47 pupils on the register of SEN and three pupils have a statement of SEN'. *In the final report, readers are not told the basis upon which the number of pupils with EAL is higher than average, and nor is pupils' ethnicity recorded. In the pre-inspection analysis, the lead inspector notes that the number of pupils from ethnic minority backgrounds is above average, and details are given of four additional languages spoken: Yoruba, Bengali, Somali, and French.*

Pre-inspection analysis

Among the issues posed by the inspection team at the end of the pre-inspection analysis are the following:

'Do all pupils make progress as well as they should on the basis of their prior attainment?'

'Are there significant variations in attainment between pupils of different gender, ethnicity, or background?'

'How well integrated are EAL pupils and do they make the progress they should?'

'To what extent do all pupils form constructive relationships and show respect for the values and attitudes of others?'

'What are the patterns of attendance in this school? Is unauthorised attendance really that low? What are the patterns of attendance among specific groups?'

By the end of inspection week, the team has acquired evidence to address each question, but the type of evidence varies in relation to each question.

Attainment

Pupils are shown to make progress on the basis of their prior attainment, but comparative statistical data illustrates that boys' attainment is lower than girls' attainment by key stage and by core subjects in comparison with national data and similar schools. Evidence is also collected to illustrate the positive steps being taken by the school to address the issue of 'boys' underachievement'.

There is an absence of monitoring data on attainment by ethnicity, so the inspection team uses a range of evidence including the headteacher's report, teacher and pupil discussion, and classroom observation to conclude that 'there are no significant differences in attainment by ethnicity'. *The meanings that might apply to the term 'no significant difference' and whether the term applies to all ethnic minority groups, including white, is not specified. Illustrative evidence is not given.*

EAL

The final report makes reference to pupils with EAL and positive judgements about the effect of a local fluency project. Positive references are also made to the first stages of implementing the National Literacy Strategy, upon attainment in English overall. *There is a tendency to conflate issues of SEN and EAL.* Thus 'the progress of pupils for whom English is an additional language is sound overall, but when they receive support from specialist staff, they make good progress. Pupils with Special Educational Needs make good progress because of effective support and provision. Lower attaining pupils make sound progress as they are usually supported by primary helpers who work sensitively with them'.

Data on the relationship between in-class support and withdrawal from classes remains unspecified. But illustrative evidence is given about the ways in which 'their [pupils'] cultures are valued'. An example given is the way in which local concerns are linked to issues of racism and to human and animal rights in classroom work.

Constructive relationships

According to the pre-inspection analysis, there has been recorded evidence of 'incidences of bullying', including one complaint in the previous report about 'racial bullying'. This is noted, and investigated during the week of inspection: the evidence base notes incidents of poor behaviour linked to pupils with SEN, no incidents of bullying, courteous behaviour to visitors, and that 'naughty pupils were seen outside the head's office'.

The final report concludes: 'Pupils are well behaved apart from a handful of pupils who have behavioural difficulties and who can disrupt the class in which they work. The school is handling this well. Pupils are generally positive when working. Although attendance is satisfactory, a significant number of pupils arrive late to school, often by up to fifteen minutes or even longer. This disrupts not only their learning but that of others'.

Despite the absence of equal opportunities and behavioural management policy documents noted in the pre-inspection analysis, the inspection team finally reports that the behaviour and attitudes of the school promote positive values. A few pupils do not behave the way they should but the school 'is handling this well'.

Attendance

Attendance record keeping is described as 'unsatisfactory'. 'When poor punctuality is taken into account, [attendance] is unsatisfactory overall. Some absences are due to pupils who are absent for extended periods during the year. For the majority of children, absences are caused by the usual childhood illnesses...Unauthorised absences are shown as being below the national average. This is incorrect and does not represent the true position.'

Findings

The main findings of the report record the following:

'What the school does well:

–   Effective leadership has led to improvements in mathematics and English

–   Provision for cultural and social development is good and for moral development is very good

- Provision for children with SEN is good

- Provision in the nursery is good and pupils make good progress

- Pupils are well-behaved and relationships are good

- Pupils have positive attitudes to work and the ethos is good'

'Where the school has weaknesses:

- Provision for information technology

- Higher attaining pupils do not make the progress they should apart from in mathematics and English

- Daily planning in all subjects, except English and mathematics, lacks detail and assessment is inconsistent throughout the school, except in mathematics

- A significant number of pupils is late to school each day

- The school does not significantly monitor the quality of its provision

- Statutory requirements for collective worship and appraisal are not met.'

'Appropriate and successful action has been taken to improve performance in some significant areas and the school provides a safe and caring ethos in which pupils can develop their personal skills.' *The key issues for action address the school's weaknesses as identified by inspectors.*

Analysis of published inspection reports

Having considered a range of issues linked to OFSTED documents and inspection processes, we undertook a detailed analysis of thirty reports and we provide supporting illustrative evidence, as appropriate, in the boxes, figures 5.4 – 5.14. For the purposes of this chapter, we focus upon six questions:

What kind of school is this?

What are the educational standards achieved?

How good are the curriculum opportunities offered to all pupils?

To what extent does teaching meet the needs of pupils for whom English is an additional language?

How well do schools care for their pupils?

Do reports present evidence on the effectiveness of a school's partnership with parents and the community?

What kind of school is this?

Pupils' ethnic composition: how important is accurate, concise and factual data?

We found no consistency in the reporting of the ethnic composition of the pupil population. The most detailed descriptions were found in the London borough which had a larger than 'average' proportion of pupils from ethnic minorities, but inconsistency was compounded by a range of qualitative and quantitative expressions of ethnicity, and a confusing, imprecise, and occasionally misleading use of ethnic composition data. In some reports, numerical referencing was omitted altogether, and qualitative terms were used in association with number – 'about', 'around', 'approximately', 'some', 'between x% and y%', as illustrated in Figure 5.4.

Responses to questions like those posed in Figure 5.4 are critically important in making accurate judgements about the extent to which the school is meeting the needs of all its pupils, and of specific groups, for example, pupils for whom English is an additional language.

FIGURE 5.4 Characteristics of a school: some confusing descriptors

A secondary school in LEA2 provides an illustrative example. Readers of the final report learn that:

'Some 13% of pupils come from families of ethnic minority origin [nos. on roll = 1375], 198 pupils coming from homes where English is not the first language. This is a higher proportion than in most schools.'

Where numbers and percentage data are mixed, meanings become unclear. What does 'some 13%' actually mean? If readers calculate the answer on the basis of the numbers on roll (1375), the answer is between 178 and 179 pupils.

Is it the case that, in addition to this number, a further '198 pupils come from homes where English is not the first language'? What is the overlap between the two groups? Are there 19 or 20 pupils in the school who come from homes where English is not the first language but not from families of ethnic minority origin?

Does the sentence mean that the pupils have English as an additional language or that their families have English as an additional language?

Is the descriptor 'pupils from families of ethnic minority origin' the same as 'ethnic minority pupils' or are other meanings being ascribed?

On what basis is the judgement being made that the number 198 is higher than in most schools, and, if we knew, what would be the implications for inspection?

Further examples of imprecision are highlighted in figure 5.5. Overall, our evidence confirms that schools do not accurately record the ethnic composition of their pupils and/or that inspectors do not consider the issue important enough to press for accuracy in the documentation they are given and upon which they are subsequently required to make judgements and compile reports. The latter explanation is equally worrying.

FIGURE 5.5 Examples of inaccurate and misleading terminology in inspection reports

Approximations

Approximately 114 children come from homes where English is not the first language (LEA1 sc2).

Just over 40% of children come from homes where English is not the first language. (LEA1 sc1).

Between 30% to 40% of the school's population is minority ethnic (LEA 1 sc6).

Some 13% of pupils come from families of ethnic minority origin (LEA2 sc6).

The school has no significant ethnic minority representation (LEA3 sc7).

Mixing words and numbers

The percentage of pupils from ethnic minorities is 41% [total numbers on roll = 579], which is high compared to national averages.

Approximately 114 pupils come from homes where English is not the first language. The main languages spoken are Chinese, French, Yoruba and Vietnamese. (LEA1 sc2)

Avoiding statistics

The intake represents a cross-section of families from varying social backgrounds and numerous ethnic minority groups...About 1/3 of the pupils come from ethnic minority backgrounds. About 1 in 8 pupils come from homes where English is not the first language. (LEA1 sc3)

Comparative terminology

The school's growing gender-balanced intake [nos. on roll = 388] contains a lower than average proportion of children from homes where English is not the first language. (LEA2 sc6)

Does 'whiteness' matter?

Unlike other forms of ethnic classification, white ethnicity was not problematised. In seven schools, ethnicity was invisible. No account was given of ethnic composition, and in five of those schools there was no mention of pupils for whom English is an additional language: all of these schools were located in the Midlands LEA where the school population is predominantly white (LEA3). It is not clear whether this was because the school intake was all or mainly white, although this was implicit. Readers also have to assume that in the same schools there were no pupils with EAL, since unlike SEN, EAL was not mentioned elsewhere in the reports.

In two examples only, inspectors drew readers' attention to the pre-dominance of 'whiteness'. In one case, this was to express potential educational advantage, and also to highlight its openness to pupils with 'specific' needs. Thus a primary school in the London borough is:

> located in the [M] ward and the majority of its pupils come from white, middle class, professional backgrounds. However, the school reviewed its admissions policy in 1989 and now provides six open places for pupils with special educational, medical, or social needs [pupils on roll = 172]. Approximately 10% of pupils come from ethnic minority backgrounds, mainly Afro-Caribbean. A very small percentage of pupils comes from families where English is not the first language.

Features such as pupil bilingualism, ethnic diversity and racial harmony were not generally seen as appropriate in school descriptions, although 'diversity' was identified as a positive aspect of the quality of education achieved in most of the schools located in the London borough. Exceptionally, the identification of racial harmony as a school characteristic was noted in a secondary school in a London borough where:

> between 30 to 40% of the school's population is minority ethnic, with Black African and African Caribbean pupils being the largest minority group. There is a strong sense of racial harmony in the school.

Ethnicity as a problem

Commonly, ethnic minority pupil populations were itemised alongside the potential for disadvantage. Occasionally a small minority group became a potential advantage and took on a particular significance. Thus a Catholic secondary school in an expanding town in the South of England:

> is the only Catholic secondary school in [LEA2] and attracts pupils not only from the whole of [LEA2] but also from the surrounding areas. The arrangements that this school has made to welcome a small group of Chinese pupils is characteristic of this school's determination to respond to individual needs.

Classifications of ethnic minority groups were also problematic and showed variation, especially in relation to the terms Black, Black African, African Caribbean, and Afro-Caribbean, and the very general classification 'Asian'. An illustrative case is a special school in LEA2. Here, it is not just that the numbers were inaccurate as stated, or that such classifications were unhelpful in the absence of further data, but it was also considered acceptable to categorise one pupil as 'other'. The school was described as a:

> mixed, day, special school for children and young people aged 2 to 19 with severe learning difficulties [nos. on roll = 98 f/t and 8 p/t]...Six pupils come from homes where English is not the first language: two are Bangladeshi, one is Chinese, two are Black Caribbean, one is Indian and there is one classified as 'other'.

English as an additional language: more than descriptive 'sloppiness'

The phrase 'pupils for whom English is an additional language' was also used as a way of describing the characteristics of a school. We will refer to specific curriculum opportunities in a later section, but note here the various descriptors applied to such pupils, sometimes in tandem with pupils' ethnicity, as in a secondary school in LEA2 where:

> Nearly 9% [nos. on roll = 1425] come from families of ethnic minority background and many of these families do not use English as their first language.

Reference was made to pupils who spoke English as an additional Language, to homes or families where English was an additional language, to parents who spoke English as an additional language, and pupils without English as their mother tongue. The issue amounts to more than descriptive sloppiness. Different descriptors have a range of meanings and imply different kinds of needs and a range of institutional responses which ought to be subject to inspection. The lack of precision raises important questions about the extent to which inspection teams had the expertise, knowledge and skills to make judgements about the strategies in place to meet pupils' needs in school. This was particularly evident in reports where issues of SEN and EAL were conflated. 'First' languages were identified in only three reports. No reports identified the ethnic composition of pupils with SEN and/or with statements of SEN.

Overall:

Our analysis demonstrates vagueness in the reporting of ethnic composition as an aspect of school characteristics.

The lack of precision raises questions about how effectively inspectors could make full and accurate judgements elsewhere in the report about the extent to which a school was meeting the needs of all its pupils.

There was evidence of omissions and anomalies in the ways that schools recorded ethnic composition. This raises concerns about the extent to which schools were monitoring and/or were able to monitor and evaluate the progress of pupils from different ethnic groups.

We noted a disinclination to focus upon ethnic diversity as a positive characteristic of a school and/or to ignore ethnic composition altogether in all or predominantly white schools.

The evidence calls into question the reliability and validity of OFSTED reports as the basis for comparative nationwide analyses of attainment and/or achievement data by ethnicity for benchmarking purposes.

What are the educational standards achieved?
Lack of statistical information

Reports prioritised attainment data by key stage, by examinations, and by gender. Data was given on the numbers of pupils with SEN, those on the SEN register and those eligible for free school meals. Comparison was made with national averages and similar schools, and other descriptors like 'other shire counties'.

Attainment data by key stage or by examination was not recorded by ethnicity. With the exception of the two special schools, attainment data on pupils with EAL was not given. Judgements were, therefore, mainly dependent upon data collection during inspection and school/ headteacher documents. For all these reasons, judgements about attainment among ethnic minority groups were expressed mainly in qualitative terms. The outcomes were qualitative judgements ex-

---

FIGURE 5.6 Examples of qualitative data relating to ethnicity from inspection reports

The following extracts are from an inspection report of a secondary school situated in a 'shire county'. The reader learns that:

'Racial harmony is the norm' and

'Pupils from ethnic minorities hold their own and some reach high standards.'

The meaning of 'holding their own' is not clarified. It is not specified how or why pupils from ethnic minorities should not/might not be 'holding their own', nor to which ethnic minorities the term might apply, nor what might be happening in the case of pupils who might not 'be holding their own'. In the absence of attainment data for different ethnic minority groups in the school, readers are left to guess the meaning of 'high standards'. Elsewhere in the report it is noted that:

'No formal work has yet been done to monitor the attainment of pupils from ethnic minorities, nor that of boys and girls separately.'

The meaning of 'no formal work' is not developed, but there is another reference in the report to:

'Pupils from different ethnic backgrounds [who] work harmoniously. They appreciate working together as part of a group and respond maturely to challenges, for instance in collaborative tasks.'

In the educational standards section an earlier phrase is repeated:

'Lesson observation and the study of written work indicate little variation in the latter and clear evidence that ethnic minority pupils easily hold their own.'

---

pressed in vague and occasionally disturbing ways. Figure 5.6 provides an illustrative example.

Equalities: a 'key issue for action'?

A key feature of reports was the invisibility of equalities issues in the 'Key Issues for Action', even where variations in attainment were highlighted elsewhere in the report. Moreover, where judgements about limited progress in relation to pupils' cultural developments in school *did* feature as a prioritised 'Key Issue for Action', this did not appear to affect overall judgements about a school's effectiveness. Figures 5.7 and 5.8 provide examples of these phenomena.

FIGURE 5.7 Variations in attainment by ethnicity – no cause for action?

The following extracts are from a secondary school located in a London borough (LEA1). Readers learn that the school is:

'a welcoming and happy school with many good features. These have contributed to increasing popularity in recent years. Its community ethos fosters a secure and frequently stimulating learning environment for the majority of its pupils. Staff are committed to the school's improvement, working harmoniously with pupils, parents, and governors.'

Yet:

'There are variations in the attainment of different ethnic groups within the school' [and this is developed in under separate subject headings].

Despite this:

there are no specific key issues for action that relate to attainment issues among different ethnic groups. Instead, key issues are couched in terms of 'the need for improvement for all'.

FIGURE 5.8 Preparation for a multicultural society – a marginal concern?

The following extracts are from a secondary school in an expanding town in the south of England (LEA2).

Overall, judgements about the school are 'very good', notwithstanding that

'cultural development is unevenly promoted, particularly in relation to preparation for life in a culturally diverse society'

and where key issues for action include:

'the need to focus upon more general improvements in performance... the need for an improved focus upon preparing pupils better for life in a culturally diverse society.'

Isolation of equalities issues

As importantly, equality of opportunity issues were judged as if they were not aspects of interest for all sections of the report. Instead, judgements about race equality were made in isolation. Thus a secondary school in LEA2 was judged to provide 'equality of opportunity and access for all pupils' even where judgements in other sections clearly indicated otherwise. This is illustrated in Figure 5.9, and raises a number of issues, including the priority given to race equality, the quality of liaison among the inspection team during inspection week, and/or the emphasis given by the lead inspector to equality of opportunity.

FIGURE 5.9 Examples of a report where equality means inequality

The following extracts are from a secondary school in LEA2, where the judgement in the final report is that 'there is equality of opportunity and access for all pupils.'

Yet:

'In the current year 8, the first year for pupils in the school, one in three of the pupils has identified SEN. They make insufficient progress...'

'The quality of teaching is monitored well by managers, but does not yet clearly identify ways to improve achievement in all cases. The learning needs of the pupils are sometimes not matched well to the tasks and approaches used in the lessons. Teachers do not always give pupils good guidance on how to improve their work.'

'There are many instances in the school of teaching and guidance which develop pupils' spiritual and cultural knowledge and understanding but these are not planned to ensure that there is a full experience, presented in a coherent way for all pupils.'

When in doubt, use 'significant'

In the expression of judgements about the educational attainment and achievement of ethnic minority groups, terms like 'significant' and 'noticeable' recurred frequently. It is unclear whether such terms are being applied quantitatively or qualitatively, and, as importantly, what inferences might be drawn from such statements. Accordingly where an inspection team in a secondary school report judged there to be 'a significant number of boys from ethnic minority origins who achieve very high standards', we need to ask:

How many is a significant number?

Should the reader be surprised? Why?

What did the 'other' ethnic minority boys attain?

What did the ethnic minority girls attain?

What did the ethnic minority boys attain relative to all boys or to all girls or to all pupils in the school?

If there was more than one ethnic group, how did the attainment of one group of boys compare to that of (an)other group(s)?

What meaning is being applied to 'very high standards'? How is this translated into 'actual' attainment and achievement?

How good are the curriculum opportunities offered to all pupils?

An inspection team is required to evaluate how curriculum planning takes account of age, capacity, gender, ethnicity and background, competence in English as an additional language and special educational needs. Judgements are also required on the extent to which the curriculum provides equality of access and opportunities for all pupils, and how the school's organisation contributes to achieving those ends. All of the above includes the extent to which a school addresses the needs of its most vulnerable groups and individuals.

The rationale for a 'cultural' curriculum

There was little evidence from the reports to suggest that judgements were being made about the extent to which the curriculum was equipping pupils with the skills to prevent, recognise and combat racism. Rather, inspectors tended to make judgements about the extent to which some curriculum subjects contribute to 'cultural awareness'. Specific examples of effective practice were highlighted. These were expressed in very similar ways, frequently in relation to subjects like art, music and religious education.

Mathematics and science were rarely singled out for 'cultural' comment. Less positive comments about attention to culturally diverse approaches and materials, particularly in relation to 'pupils' cultural development', were found mainly in LEA2 and LEA3. Reports confirmed that in some schools there was little awareness of the extent to which pupils lived in multicultural communities. In other words, inspectors were sometimes blind to the demography of an area. Homogeneity was assumed because the school was predominantly white, even when the town was culturally diverse. Further, some inspection judgements suggested a similar lack of awareness among inspectors. In a shire county secondary school, for example, judgements were made on the basis of the pupils' 'own cultural traditions' as compared with the cultural traditions of 'non-European cultures', expressed as if *multi*cultural communities did not exist:

> Good opportunities are provided for pupils to develop an appreciation of their own cultural traditions through subjects, especially art, music, the humanities and English, as well as through a wide variety of cross-curricular activities... However, an awareness of non-European cultures is limited, and ways of improving the preparation of pupils for life in a culturally diverse society should be developed throughout the curriculum.

In the above example, inspectors draw a sharp distinction between the pupils' 'own cultural traditions', implying that these are exclusively European and failing to note that much of popular music, for example, draws on a range of non-European cultural traditions. 'Non-European cultures' are portrayed as something separate and 'other' whereas the reality is more complex, and even in relatively homogeneous communities, individuals wittingly or unwittingly experience multiculturalism on a daily basis through the media and as consumers.

In other examples, references to multicultural or anti-racist curricula were effectively side-stepped by the preferred use of other terms like 'cultural education'. In one secondary school, for example, inspectors reported that:

> Cultural education is well developed in some parts of the school...There is good coverage of these issues in art, history and religious education but weaknesses in maths, science and music...Cultural education is limited to food technology in design and technology.

Elsewhere, the reports contained many subject-specific references to learning about other cultures and reflected a strong emphasis upon

---

FIGURE 5.10 Learning about other cultures

'In a number of subjects, pupils develop their respect for the beliefs and values of others, although this is not a sufficiently strong feature of religious education, particularly.'

'Pupils are given a wide range of opportunities to learn about their own and other cultures through a number of subjects. In music, for example, pupils listen to Chinese music and deepen their understanding by making their own compositions in character.'

'In physical education pupils learn about fair play and facing defeat as well as success in competitive sport and in religious education pupils encounter the evils of slavery and racial persecution.'

'The last inspection noted that the school had not yet developed a curriculum that reflected the cultural diversity of British society but much had been done to rectify this. For instance, the music and art departments make excellent provision for pupils to explore the cultures of Africa, India, China, and Japan as well as encouraging pupils in the understanding and enjoyment of the culture of the western world. Pupils learn to appreciate a diversity of different foods and are able to discover the significance of religious festivals such as Diwali.'

'Art – the range of artists chosen for study does not take enough account of the need to represent artists of both genders from a variety of cultures.'

---

cultural knowledge. In Figure 5.10 we provide illustrative examples from five inspection reports.

'Cultural education' and school effectiveness

The impact of judgements about cultural awareness upon overall judgements about a school's effectiveness, or more general statements about curriculum provision, was not always clear. Thus, even in a secondary school where cultural provision was judged to be 'good', 'the wide range of local cultural traditions is not used sufficiently to develop pupils' understanding and enjoyment of cultural diversity'.

and

'Preparation for life in a multicultural society [was] less in evidence.'

Equally importantly, weaknesses in providing a culturally diverse curriculum appeared to have minimal impact upon overall judgements about the educational standards achieved or the quality of education provided. This point is reinforced by the interviews with headteachers (see chapter six). Their perspective was that judgements about culturally diverse provision were low in terms of inspection priorities.

Overall:

The curriculum issues prioritised by inspectors reflected a historical view of multiculturalism in which the pervasive assumption is that exposure to knowledge and content about diverse communities, 'other' cultures and 'other' ways of life are all that is needed to combat racism.

It is equally significant that weaknesses in provision, even in the limited terms stated above, appeared to have little overall effect upon judgements about whether schools were effective and to what degree.

To what extent does teaching meet the needs of pupils for whom English is an additional language?

Earlier in this chapter we noted how 'the number of pupils for whom English is an additional language' was used as a characteristic of the school, sometimes linked to data on ethnic composition and sometimes to pupils with special educational needs. Overall, 15 out of 30 reports made references to EAL in the *school characteristics* sections. This is a higher proportion than in the OFSTED-based text search, in which references to EAL were found in 35.9 per cent of reports between 1997-1999 (see Appendix item 6).

Limited focus and attention

We found that limited focus was given to EAL in the relevant aspect sections of the report and in the section on English, and there was almost no evidence of attention given to differential attainment and progress between monolingual and bilingual groups or between different ethnic minority groups.

Throughout the reports, few consistent patterns emerged in the references made to EAL. References to EAL were at times notable by their absence. For example, in a London borough primary school where 'between 30 to 40% of the school population is minority ethnic', detailed accounts were given of 'SEN provision ...of the highest order' but no mention was made of EAL provision, despite the fact that the school drew on a catchment area where many residents are bilingual.

Where judgements were made, they were expressed in standardised formats, and when these were identified in the main findings, they did not always recur as a 'Key Issue for Action'. A judgement from an urban secondary school report that 'the needs of pupils with English as an additional language are not adequately identified or sufficiently supported' was missing from the *Key Issues for Action*. Instead, the school was required to 'continue to raise standards to meet the needs of pupils of all abilities, especially in the areas of maths and English'. An exceptional case was found in LEA2, where a key issue for action in a secondary school included the need for: 'in-service training...to update staff in teaching non-English speakers, and for all support staff to develop further their knowledge and use of appropriate teaching strategies when supporting the learning of pupils for whom English is an Additional Language'.

SEN or EAL?

Some pupils for whom English is an additional language may also have special educational needs, but others do not. This issue was not always made clear; in some reports, EAL was absorbed into reporting sections on SEN issues, and there were examples of generalised statements in which the two were conflated, as in the following example from a primary school in a London borough:

> There are no significant differences in attainment measured against gender, ethnicity or background. Pupils with SEN and those for whom EAL achieve satisfactory and sometimes good standards relative to their individual targets.

Invisibility took other forms. For example, in LEA3, a shire county, one secondary school was recorded in the *school characteristics* section of the report as having seven pupils for whom English is an additional language. Subsequently they disappeared from the evidence base, since no further mention was made elsewhere in the report about those pupils and whether their specific language needs were being met.

Support in classrooms and withdrawal strategies

Finally, where guidance to inspectors (OFSTED, 1999f) focuses upon the importance of observing pupils with EAL both in classrooms and in small group support work, there was limited illustrative evidence about the rigour or consistency with which this was accomplished. Analysis did not include judgements about the appropriateness of withdrawal from their curricular activities. It was not always possible to unravel the extent to which inspection judgements had been made partly or wholly on the basis of whether pupils were withdrawn from classes to receive specific additional support, or whether a preference and, if so, in precisely what circumstances, was given to in-class support. The nature of support for pupils was not always specified. In Figure 5.11 a range of examples demonstrate that the precise nature of the support and its purposes needs more clarification, as does the evidence base upon which inspectors judge 'good' practice.

FIGURE 5.11 Examples of the need for greater clarification in relation to EAL provision

'A small number of pupils for whom English is an additional language are currently given additional help. Usefully, this is separate from provision for SEN support and is closely linked to the English department. As necessary, pupils are withdrawn for specific teaching.'

'Pupils for whom English is an additional language make progress when they receive adequate support. Some pupils receive inadequate support and fail to make enough progress to reach higher stages of fluency and competency in English.'

'The school is a centre for the education of students with SEN. The proportion of pupils with statements is one of the highest for mainstream schools in the country. (*No figures are provided in the report to substantiate this claim*). 'Many more students require and receive additional learning support. Nearly 9% of students come from ethnic minority origin and many of these pupils do not use English as their first language.'

'The school has made good provision to respond to the specific needs of a significant group of Chinese students whose personal needs are met well...So far, specific teaching approaches to meet the needs of learners for whom English is a second language are still developing.'

Overall:

We found reporting in this area to be very variable, with an over-dependence on generalised statements and a narrow focus. Our findings reinforce a view of EAL provision as an area in which the specific expertise of inspectors is often not apparent from their reports.

How well do schools care for their pupils?

Here our analysis focused upon: measures recorded to promote good attendance and behaviour and to eliminate oppressive behaviour including bullying; pupils' moral development; the explicit identification of moral, social, cultural and spiritual issues in schools' aims and values; and pupils' personal development. Reports also address exclusions, attendance, and punctuality.

Exclusions

Each report included exclusions data; of the thirty reports, only three record exclusions by pupils' ethnic background and by gender. Judgements about whether some groups were over-represented were absent from all the reports. No report provided action points concerning the promotion of policies and practices for inclusion.

A disturbing aspect of our data was the discrepancy in judgements about what constituted 'high' or 'low' levels of exclusion, and about exclusions being negative or positive features of schools' behavioural management practices and in what circumstances. 'Low' levels or no exclusions were not judged to be worth commenting upon at all.

Positive judgements about exclusions were linked to the maintenance of good behavioural management policies, in particular, strategies to combat bullying. Figures 5.12 and 5.13 provide illustrative examples of the way in which exclusions data were embedded into wider strategies for behaviour management. In Figure 5.13, declining numbers of exclusions were seen as positive. This was the only example among the published school inspection reports we examined in which we found an explicit discussion of strategies to deal with racial discrimination.

FIGURE 5.12 Links between exclusions data and judgements about behaviour management

The following extracts are from a secondary school located in a fast expanding urban environment (LEA2). Readers learn that:

'There is no evidence of racial disharmony, pupils sit and work collaboratively in varied groups of mixed gender and ethnicity. Pupils listen to one another, share opinions and respect the views of others.'

'A clear anti-bullying code applies, and, whilst a few instances of harassing behaviour arise, response is swift, thorough and unequivocal. The school employs fixed term exclusion [185 in previous year]...as part of a planned process to support discipline and to good effect.' [*No indications are given about the type of harassing behaviour*].

'Pupils understand the difference between right and wrong...'

'The introduction of electronic communications systems across the school is beginning to contribute to individual and group support strategies by ensuring that staff are notified of progress or causes of concern rapidly. Pupils recognise the mechanisms in place around them to provide guidance and support and can clearly identify the benefit of these to themselves.' [*Again, no specific data is given of why individual and group support strategies might be needed, and in which circumstances*].

FIGURE 5.13 Examples of positive behaviour management in a school with declining numbers of pupil exclusions

The following extracts are from a secondary school also located in LEA2, as above. Readers learn that:

'Students and teachers are very well aware of equal opportunities issues. The practices reflect the strong commitment to the values of respect and tolerance of others. There is an equal opportunities statement and in matters of access to the curriculum, gender, ability, and race are well addressed in many departments.'

'Girls and boys are treated equally by their teachers...Other issues relating to equality of opportunity and to social and racial discrimination are dealt with in a most careful and sensitive manner.'

'The respectful, secure and orderly community atmosphere of the school makes a real contribution to students' standards of achievement....Students indicate little concern about bullying and believe that any incidents are dealt with effectively...The school's high temporary exclusion rate is now declining' [*92 in the previous year*].

'There is a palpable expectation that pupils behave in a moral way. Fair and positive rewards and sanctions, and the examples set by adults in the school, make positive contributions to students' moral and social development. The quality of students' welfare and guidance is a strength of the school.'

Harassment and bullying

References to strategies for dealing with bullying were common to all reports. Reference to *racial* bullying or harassment was made in two reports only. The tendency was for judgements to rest on whether schools had procedures in place to deal with bullying or harassment, and how effective the policy was judged to be in practice. Since inspectors' judgements were made out of context, it was impossible to ascertain whether any harassment or bullying that did occur was racially motivated or not. If racial harassment or bullying was occurring, it was largely invisible to readers, as in the following example:

> the school's policies effectively encourage good standards of behaviour and incidents of harassment and bullying are rare. When they occur they are dealt with appropriately.

Behavioural issues

With the exception of the one school for which special measures had been recommended, behaviour management problems usually centred on a 'minority' of pupils who were presenting behavioural problems. However, it was not always made clear which characteristics such pupils shared, other than a propensity to behave less well than the 'majority'. So we find these comments in two primary schools' reports, from LEA1 and LEA2 respectively:

> Pupils are well behaved apart from a handful of pupils who have behavioural difficulties. The school is handling this well.

> Most pupils have a positive attitude to learning. Most co-operate with their teachers... but there is, however, some restlessness and lack of attention in some classes in both key stages.

In classroom observation data, behavioural issues were linked to teachers' strategies as well as to pupils' behaviour. The following examples from three primary school reports illustrate this, and in two of them reference is made also to parents – their particular concerns or their awareness of the school's policy (see also below).

> Measures are in place to promote discipline and good behaviour, although some members of staff need more support if they are to maintain good levels of behaviour and learning. The school has a clear

definition of bullying, and, despite the concerns of a small number of parents, all incidents are dealt with sensitively.

Behaviour is mostly good in class, though it deteriorates where there is poor class management by some short term supply teachers and by some permanent teachers.

The school has a clear code of conduct which is promoted in the school prospectus and understood and supported by parents. Some ground rules are established early on in the under-fives so that pupils are clear about expectations for their conduct and behaviour....However, on some occasions where the school's behaviour policy is not implemented effectively by teachers, some pupils take advantage of the situation and misbehave.

Do reports present evidence on the effectiveness of a school's partnership with parents and the community?

Parents: a uniform body?

We found that the section of the reports addressing schools' partnerships with parents showed much similarity and were often brief. Parents were most usually discussed as if they were a homogeneous body with uniform needs. Commentaries on the parents' questionnaire were brief, although identified issues did appear in other sections of the report. There was no evidence in the reports to suggest that low attendance at the parents' evening might be an issue upon which to report. There were few indications that there were a range of parent communities for whom a variety of approaches and strategies might be needed in order to foster more effective home-school communication. The only exceptions were inspection reports from the London borough. Where diversity was recognised, comments were often linked to strategies for improving written communication with parents. Statements like 'the school has introduced a range of measures to encourage Asian [sic] parents into the school' require further development and explanation if they are to constitute meaningful judgements about school-parent partnerships.

Community

The term 'community' was used in a variety of ways, sometimes referring to specific people such as the local police officer or dentist. In some reports it was linked to much broader concepts like the 'environment', the 'local community', or 'local industry'. In a minority of the reports examined, relations with the local community were judged as needing 'improvement'. The need for improvement in relation to pupils' cultural development was also linked to the 'wider community', and it was in this context that references were made to the need for greater awareness about living in a culturally diverse or multicultural society. However, such judgements were expressed so generally that they raised questions about the extent to which schools might usefully act on them. Some illustrative examples of community focus are shown as Figure 5.14.

FIGURE 5.14 Judgements about school and community relationships

[The school's] 'community ethos fosters a secure and frequently stimulating environment, working harmoniously with parents, community and governors'. (LEA1 secondary school)

'The school has few links with the community or religious organisations.' (LEA1 secondary school)

'The school should seek to strengthen its partnership with parents and the local community.' (LEA1 secondary school)

'Parents are made to feel welcome in the school. There are numerous visits from the local community, including a local policeman who is assisting in the year 6 pupils obtaining a citizenship award.' (LEA2 primary school)

'The involvement of parents in the school is outstanding, Whilst there is little direct involvement by local industry and business, the school has an impressive record of involvement in the local community.' (LEA2 primary school)

'The use of the immediate and local environment is a great strength.' (LEA3 special school)

Overview

- A pervasive feature of the inspection reports analysed was the standardised nature of the language and format. Schools provided 'satisfactory', 'sound', 'good', or 'very good' 'value for money'. If a school did not reach 'satisfactory' in accordance with most of the judgement criteria, it was judged as needing 'special measures'. Except for the one school in the latter category, all schools had 'strengths' which 'outweighed' their 'weaknesses', and both these and 'key issues for action' were expressed qualitatively. In the final reports, overall judgements applied a language that rarely prioritised issues of race or addressed attainment by specific ethnic groups. Although differentials in attainment were identified in the text of some reports, the tendency was for such issues to become hidden in stock phrases like 'the need to raise improvement for all' or the need for improved recognition of 'cultural diversity' in a school's curriculum. This was especially the case in the section of the report dealing with the *Main Findings* and *Key Issues for Action.*

• The 'key indicators' provide the main source of statistical data; among the more recent reports analysed this was presented in a comparative form with national averages, similar schools, and all schools. Key stage, test and examination results provided the main source of comparative data. None of the inspection reports commented on any differentials in attainment by ethnicity.

• The term race equality was absent from the reports. Our findings were supported by an OFSTED-based text search for the term race equality in 10,623 reports between 1997 and 1999, where race equality or racial equality is found in only 0.25 per cent of the reports (see Appendix item 6). Elements of race equality were implicit in the concept of equal opportunities, mostly in relation to access. Equality of opportunity was embedded in the reports but did not constitute a prime focus. Equality of opportunity did not usually encompass race equality. In relation to the reports examined, the concerns central to this research were implicit rather than explicit. Race equality was generally marginal and often wholly absent.

• Data on ethnicity was applied inconsistently. Critically, precise numerical data on the ethnic composition of pupil populations were significantly lacking. Where ethnic data was used, this was most frequently to define the characteristics of a school and its catchment area, rather than to consider pupils' attainment, achievements or progress. Without precise data, evidence that ethnic minority pupils 'hold their own' or that 'some reach very high standards' were relatively meaningless judgements. It thus was difficult to establish the extent to which a school, or its curriculum, matched the needs of its pupils.

- A general assumption was that good practice for individual pupils was good practice for all pupils. There were no judgements of the extent to which structural inequalities were being experienced by specific groups of pupils in a school. This suggests that such concerns might also have been absent from the conceptual and operational schema within which individual inspectors and inspection teams operated.

- No information was provided on the ethnicity of pupils with special educational needs (SEN). There were, however, links made between judgements about pupils with EAL and pupils with SEN. The rationale for these links was not always transparent, and the focus upon EAL was limited.

- Ethnic composition data related almost entirely to pupils rather than adults. In the reports sampled, only one report (in LEA1) noted the development of a school's staffing policy to reflect its pupil constituency; another inspection report noted efforts to encourage more 'Asian' parents into school. The need for, or expectations of, staff development regarding equal opportunities or of staff recruitment to 'match' pupil composition were non-issues in the reports sampled.

- The curriculum issues prioritised by inspectors reflected an outdated view of multiculturalism, according to which it is assumed that exposure to knowledge and content about diverse communities, 'other' cultures, and 'other' ways of life will prevent and address racism.

- Specific judgements about curricula to combat racism were not given, although mention of 'racism' as a topic for classroom discussion was referenced in five reports.

- In relation to pupils' moral and social development, inspectors did emphasise the importance of policies to eliminate all forms of oppressive behaviour including harassment and bullying. Specific reference to race and ethnicity was found most commonly in school reports for LEA1, the London borough. In this LEA racism, tolerance, success, failure and prejudice were more likely to be discussed as subject-focused aspects of the curriculum and considered in a range of subjects such as English, drama, art and music, and in religious or physical education. Such concepts were not generally linked to pupils' moral development.

- Bullying was assumed to have common rather than distinctive causes and 'racial bullying' was rarely referenced. Although inspectors highlighted preventative measures to combat bullying and schools' procedures for responding to it, they tended not to report on the effectiveness of specific measures.

- The needs of pupils with English as an additional language were not always addressed coherently. The distinction between pupils with special educational needs and those for whom English is an additional language was not always clear. In the absence of precise evidence from the inspection reports, it is difficult for a reader to establish the extent to which sufficient and appropriate EAL support is being given. It is also difficult to assess the impact of a school's provision on pupils' performance.

- Bilingualism was rarely noted as an asset or a cause for celebration. Linked to EAL issues and ethnic minority support, bilingualism was most commonly presented as a problem that required both a solution(s) and/or remediation by schools. Reports showed inconsistency in approaches towards pupil withdrawal from mainstream classes; comments were positive when the quality of teaching and learning in withdrawal groups was considered to be satisfactory or above, and positive also when adequate support was given in the classroom. There was no evidence of inspection judgements about time limits for withdrawal work. Regular reviews and individual plans of work for pupils with EAL (where noted) and SEN were sometimes emphasised as positive features of schools' work.

Conclusions

The inspection framework in place between 1996 and 1999 had the potential to make a key contribution to OFSTED's lead responsibility to prevent and address racism in schools. Through the publication and interpretation of attainment data, inspection teams could focus on the relative attainment of minority groups and ways of promoting their achievement.

For both schools and inspection teams, the task of enacting a rigorous quality management system is to evaluate fully and accurately all the services schools provide to meet the needs of individual pupils and the needs of specific groups of pupils. That task is complex and challenging.

Despite attention to some aspects of race equality in the previous framework, and some re-focused attention in the new framework, this chapter suggests that there remains scope for further improvement. Inspectors will need further support, training and guidance if they are to use the current 2000 school inspection framework to promote race equality more effectively than inspectors did under the previous framework.

Chapter 6

HEADTEACHERS' PERSPECTIVES

If race equality is an important moral issue in this country then I think the OFSTED inspection framework could be explicit about this. It's not explicit in the new framework. It can't be quantified in the hard-nosed way that some data can be. But if it's an issue for society then schools could be asked how they are responding to society's agenda. Primary headteacher, after an OFSTED inspection under the current 2000 framework

This chapter reports on the perspectives of ten headteachers from schools in the three selected LEAs of our study. Five were headteachers of secondary schools, four of primary schools and one was the head of a special school. The interviews took place between January and March 2000 and all the headteachers had experienced OFSTED inspections under the previous framework. One of the ten schools had also recently been inspected under the current 2000 framework and all the headteachers had had a chance to study this new framework.

We wanted to know how headteachers understood race equality issues in relation to inspection; in particular how they understood and responded to assessments of their practice and provision for equality. We also wished to establish what headteachers identified as indicators of race equality in their schools.

Race equality on the agenda?

Preparing for inspection

We found that most of the headteachers in our study, whether they worked in culturally diverse or more homogenous and predominantly white communities, did not, prior to inspection, anticipate that equality issues generally, or race equality in particular, would be something in which the inspection team would show special interest:

> Given that OFSTED inspects absolutely everything, I had no reason to believe it wasn't an issue, but I hadn't picked it out as a particular issue of an inspection. *Primary headteacher, LEA 2*

This same headteacher went on to explain that his staff was unlikely to identify race equality as an inspection priority:

> I have to say, if I asked our staff by questionnaire, they would probably see it [race equality] as one of the lowest priorities during their inspection within this school. And if I had asked them to actually identify priorities and not given any boxes to fill in or to prioritise I think they would probably not even have put it down as a priority. *Primary headteacher, LEA 2*

Other headteachers saw race equality generally, or a specific element of their provision, as being central to their work, but felt this was not necessarily reflected in the interests of the inspection team:

> We had identified where there were English as a second language needs and that they were being met, and that we had a sense of the ability potential of those children. ... I mean I think it [race equality] was not central to the OFSTED process. *Secondary headteacher, LEA 2*

> Not at all. It didn't come across as a particular concern of theirs. It wasn't something that was raised much during the inspection. I suppose, without being complacent, it was one of the areas where we felt reasonably confident that we were doing a number of things that perhaps other schools were not doing. *Secondary headteacher, LEA 1*

In fact this last comment confirms the perceptions of the members of HMI, presented in chapter three, that if race equality issues are not perceived as a *problem* by contracted inspectors, they are generally not reported on in any detail. In effect, this often results in examples of good practice being omitted from reports.

Another headteacher expected that certain inequalities in provision and in the use of exclusion in his school would be raised but, in the event, the inspecting team appeared to overlook them:

> We were very conscious there would be comments on exclusions, exclusion [of pupils] from the ethnic communities, exam results, whether they were better or worse. So in that sense we were aware, but no one was specifically raising those issues with us. ... So these are things they

> [the governors] are constantly aware of – so they would detect racism. But it was certainly was not an issue that the [inspection] team raised in any kind of overt way with me. *Secondary headteacher, LEA 2*

In this last school the headteacher and governors were well aware of disparities in performance between ethnic groups, and of the disproportionate exclusion of African Caribbean boys, and had a rigorous monitoring system in place. However, the inspecting team appeared to be less concerned about this problem than the school was.

In only one case did the headteacher expect the inspection team to focus on equality and then find that they did so. This was a small village school, with a largely white middle class intake, situated in a village close to a city with an ethnically diverse population. The headteacher commented:

> I knew that equal opportunities would certainly be an issue and therefore in that would be racial issues too, but whether that was actually spelt out prior to the inspection by the Regi, I can't honestly remember. But I would imagine that she would because she was very thorough, but it was also in her mind anyway. *Primary headteacher, LEA 3*

The processes of inspection

During inspection, headteachers reported that they were not generally aware of race equality issues being looked at in any systematic way, although some inspection teams seem to focus on certain race equality issues more sharply than others do. For example:

> I know that one of the inspectors who was actually interested in geography and history actually did a check on the library stock to look at the suitability of the books there and undertook quite a wide ranging check on the stock. Clearly one of the aims was to look at any bias, racial or sexual bias. Also, I know the question was asked, he [an inspector] asked the question to T [a deputy head], because T was actually relating this to me: 'What would happen if there was a case of racial abuse, for example?' And T was able to say that the last time that something like this did happen he had reported it to the next governors' meeting. *Secondary headteacher, LEA 3*

Responding to inspection assessments

Two schools, both in LEA 2, a Midlands shire county, had responded specifically to assessments of their provision and practice for race equality. The first, a secondary school, was described by its head as:

> Middle class, but there are areas of deprivation, financial and social. But yes, you would consider it a good catchment [area, with] very supportive parents in the main, and it is increasingly becoming a popular school. *Secondary headteacher, LEA 3*

The school had, overall, a positive report but was criticised concerning pupils' spiritual development. Inspectors concluded that although pupils were aware of the many religious traditions in Britain, their understanding of Christianity, Judaism and Islam was basic. Although this did not feature in the *Key Issues for Action* section of the report, the school had addressed this weakness in its action plan.

The second school, a village primary with a predominantly, although not exclusively, white pupil population, also had a very positive inspection report. However, it was criticised for its failure to develop an appropriate multicultural curriculum. It was the only school in the sample of 30 reports which we examined, which had such a point included in the *Key Issues for Action* section of the report. As the headteacher explained:

> I don't think the report produced any useful evidence that we didn't already know, again it was fairly short – a couple of paragraphs mixed in with a whole [section on pupils'] spiritual, social, cultural [development]. So I don't think the report proved of any help. What did give us the help was the fact that it identifies an issue of action which will have to be at the forefront of our development plans for the next couple of years. *Primary headteacher, LEA 3*

The headteacher explained that although he had identified this weakness in the school's provision before the inspection, he had found it difficult to take this issue forward. This was partly because there were other competing priorities, and partly because many of the staff, governors and parents did not recognise the need for a curriculum which prepared children for life in a multicultural society. Indeed, some staff lived a relatively isolated existence and rarely travelled to the multicultural city a few miles away:

It is an interesting village, because again, just going to [the city], I mean we have got all that culture on our doorstep, but going to [the city] for anybody in the village is like a big trip. I know staff, when we suggest staff do go to town, there will be staff in the village who do not go to [the city] very often, so all that culture available in [the city] doesn't reach these parts very naturally. There are not many children get over to see the Diwali lights or go shopping in [the city] and see the whole mix of race in there. So it passes the village by to an extent. *Primary headteacher, LEA 3*

This parochial attitude made it all the more difficult, firstly, to persuade colleagues that a broader curriculum was necessary and, secondly, to adopt and use resources which reflect the ethnic diversity in the country as a whole:

I think the hardest thing for the class teacher is to think of ways of bringing in, for example, cultural links or examples. And certainly one of the things is our lack of resources. They are very typically white, sort of middle class type resources. *Primary headteacher, LEA 3*

Our analysis of school inspection reports (chapter five) demonstrates that even when such problems were highlighted by inspectors, they were rarely to be found in the *Main Findings* or *Key Issues for Action* sections of reports, which are the parts made available to parents. This school was able to act on the assessment made by inspectors precisely because this particular weakness was highlighted in this way and had to be addressed in the school's action plan. The school, working with the support of the LEA advisory service, had subsequently been able to provide training for staff and to discuss the need for these developments with parents. OFSTED's contribution was in enabling issues of race equality to be given priority within the school's action plan, by listing this concern among the *Key Issues for Action*.

Ethnic monitoring, target setting and standards

Headteachers in our sample showed varying degrees of understanding of the need for ethnic monitoring in relation to educational provision or outcomes. In a school where there were just twenty-three students from minority backgrounds, accounting for 'around three per cent' of the pupil population, the head told us he had not considered introducing ethnic monitoring and had no specific data on how these minority students were achieving:

> But if we wanted to from the database we could find out who they were. I wouldn't have a clue, with one or two exceptions, but it's not something which is kept separately. If you asked me to list or name our pupils I think I would know most of them, but I would have to think really long and hard about any pupils with ethnic origin. They are just pupils at [the school] like anyone else. I think there is one in Year 7 who is partially sighted, so she would stand out as she has to have someone with her all the time, but otherwise I would have to sit down and think. *Secondary headteacher, LEA3*

Another headteacher, from a school with 'some fifteen per cent' of ethnic minority pupils, mainly from Bangladeshi and Pakistani communities, did not mention the ethnic make-up of the school in the long description she provided for us. When asked specifically about the ethnic make-up she explained:

> We've got an incoming ethnic population at the moment, and therefore the number of students from – I mean, the school is getting more multi-ethnic, if I can put it that way. ... I think the inspection report didn't [mention ethnicity]. They didn't ask about that sort of thing. In relation to race issues, I don't think we had, anyway, a high enough proportion of students for there to be any statistical [significance], for them to actually look at. *Secondary headteacher, LEA 2*

This head was very aware of the need to monitor each individual child's progress and attainment but, again, had never considered monitoring by ethnicity. She argued that there was no problem because many minority students were academically successful:

> I mean, there are students who are from ethnic backgrounds in the top, the highflying sets, in Year 9. They're in the highest flying set in Year 9 where they ought to be. I mean, in a sense we do look at where every child ought to be. And I mean, I suppose what we, where we can get to with the target minimal grade stuff, where we've identified under-achievement, is to be looking at the reasons for that and whether the reasons for that are ethnicity or not. *Secondary headteacher, LEA 2*

Consequently, her approach to equalities in education remained focused on the individual and she was unable to identify any trends in pupil performance by ethnicity:

> Our equal opportunities approach is very much to know what the needs of every individual child are, what every individual child should be achieving and to be tracking that. *Secondary headteacher, LEA 2*

In a sense the OFSTED inspection did not challenge her to think further about race equality, since the report focused on the 'integration' of minority pupils:

> I think they were seeing the children from ethnic backgrounds [as] fairly well integrated. *Secondary headteacher, LEA 2*

Consequently, she saw the senior manager team's role in promoting race equality as one of monitoring the achievements of individuals and being particularly 'supportive' of minority students. Particularly, she added, as 'some of our staff do have a racist approach':

> One of the things is monitoring.... And being very supportive when students want to have an Eid party or, you know, when groups of students want to do something very much, making sure that they are respected and valued for doing it. And that's got to come from us and you give that leadership and then that should percolate down. *Secondary headteacher, LEA 2*

Curiously, the way this head identified the solution to the problem of teachers having 'a racist approach' was not in terms of staff training or staff discipline, but in terms of supporting students in order to help them feel valued. While the example given by the senior staff might have influenced the teachers, it was by no means clear what action might be taken if these teachers fail to learn by example.

By contrast, another headteacher in the same LEA was monitoring attainment, progress and exclusions by ethnicity but found that OFSTED inspectors showed very little interest in this data:

> To be perfectly honest, I'm not conscious of them using it at all. It would be interesting to have that kind of view in the report. I mean, there is a statement: 'nine per cent of students come from ethnic minority origin'. But that's the only statement I can recall actually. I mean, when they refer

to exclusions [and] to achievement, but they don't bring out the ethnic data we give them at all. So no, it [the report] is fairly free of racial comments about the school. *Secondary headteacher, LEA 2*

This headteacher, like his colleague in LEA 2 quoted above, placed considerable emphasis on the monitoring of student performance as part of the drive to raise standards. Both heads were engaged in setting challenging targets for their schools, and saw this as an essential aspect of their leadership role. The first head relied on individual monitoring. The second believed that monitoring by ethnicity and gender was essential, and argued that it was his personal contribution to promoting race equality in the school:

> What we are keen to see is that as an institution we have some targets to report on. So that education – they [the students] have a choice as a result of their time here. And as a school one of the biggest challenges we are facing is around achievement. How vast numbers of young people can see a point to education. There are increasing numbers here who present challenges in terms of their behaviour. Young people should be able to expand their experience here so that they have a choice in the outside world. I want young people to be able to benefit from their education here. They have to pass examinations, which is the currency in terms of having a choice. So yes, we have targets for different groups of youngsters to check that all are benefiting – monitoring by ethnicity and gender. *Secondary headteacher, LEA 2*

The inspection teams visiting these two schools both adopted an equally 'colour blind' approach in their inspection reports. It would appear that in the school where no ethnic monitoring is taking place, there is no guarantee that all groups of young people are benefiting. In both schools the OFSTED inspection process is also failing to monitor whether or not all groups are, in fact, benefiting from education and having choices opened up to them through their schooling.

A headteacher from LEA 1, a London borough, made an interesting link between equalities issues, upon which the school had received a good report, and monitoring and review, for which it was criticised. He pointed out that the collection of statistics might highlight previously undetected problems but that statistical data alone would be unlikely to provide an adequate basis for remedial action:

In terms of issues of equality, they were the things that came out with a sort of glowing epithet. Those were the things that seemed to come out well in the report: the ethos, the integration, the staffing, the policies, that bit of it seemed to come out well. The bit that was weakness, I suppose, in the inspection report, were issues around monitoring, evaluation and review of practice and around target setting, and I would say, yes, the inspection report influenced me considerably. As a result of that we appointed a new senior teacher who had a specific remit around monitoring and review. We introduced target setting into the school; we looked again at the senior staff responsibilities in order to make that part of everyone's job. ...We have become much more specific in terms of analysing scores in terms of boys, girls, and ethnicity, and now do a big report on all our exam results, analysing all of those things in those terms and then trying to look carefully at why. Although sometimes those questions of why are quite difficult to answer. What do you need to do to address the issue? And sometimes statistics don't give you a clear picture as to exactly what is wrong. *Secondary headteacher, LEA 1*

In chapter two we identified the aspects of the previous and current (2000) inspection frameworks which support race equality in schools. In particular, we noted that inspectors are now given fuller guidance on how they should describe the school in terms of ethnic composition. Under the current framework, inspectors no longer have to negotiate this description with headteachers, although they are dependent on the information provided by them. The pre-inspection forms the headteacher completes require information on the ethnic make-up of the school but does not require schools to provide a breakdown of attainment by ethnicity. Schools are required to provide a breakdown of exclusions by ethnicity – but only those exclusions over the school year preceeding the inspection. Thus OFSTED still does not require schools to engage in continuous and systematic ethnic monitoring of their educational provision or of outcomes by ethnicity.

Inspecting English as an additional language

We have noted from our interviews with HMI and with contracted inspectors, that the quality of English as an additional language (EAL) inspection may vary quite considerably among inspection teams. Each contracted team needs to appoint someone with responsibility for inspecting EAL in a school where there are 'significant' numbers of pupils with EAL needs. It is not a requirement that the inspector responsible should have any expertise in this area.

One headteacher recalled how in the inspection team which visited his school, the individual responsible for EAL was someone with a degree of expertise in this area:

> One of the inspectors in the team had a particular interest in EAL and had had some sort of senior advisory position to do with EAL. So he was a bit of an expert. I think he felt that given the numbers of EAL pupils we had ... that there was insufficient provision. He was also not convinced that there was sufficient monitoring of progression through the levels of English, nor was he convinced that the good practice as evidenced through the EAL teacher working with the pupils in small groups was necessarily carried through the curriculum. So there wasn't the policy of taking that work into all classrooms, so that all departments were aware of the best way to move EAL pupils through all the stages. He wasn't convinced that that was rigorous enough. We actually felt that in terms of our judgement, this is a bit unfair, but this is all a bit confidential. We actually had a fairly ineffective EAL department in the school and we felt that the inspector's judgements were flawed in that they took the rhetoric of the teacher and the theory of the teacher, but criticised whole school practice, while not actually looking at how that teacher influenced whole school practice. So we got a bit embittered about that part of the inspection commentary which said that. *Secondary headteacher, LEA 1*

By contrast, another school, that had not managed to identify and secure additional resources for all pupils with EAL needs, received a report which read: 'the achievement for students from families for whom English is an additional language is adequate'. The overall levels of achievement were, however, criticised by the OFSTED team, and this led the headteacher to look at specific groups. With the help of an advisory teacher from the LEA ethnic minority support service, the headteacher identified a previously hidden problem with regard to students with EAL:

> In fact it was Asian boys who were not doing as well as they might do in English. I actually found that that was because although they presented as very competent English speakers, this actually hid the fact that underneath all that they weren't very competent when it came to writing

English language. The staff perception was that they were lazy. Here is a boy who can talk to me perfectly in eloquent language but he doesn't put it down on paper. This boy is therefore too lazy to actually stretch himself. And so what we found ourselves doing then was specifically targeting those students to help them, because clearly they didn't have the skills that staff perceived them to have. *Secondary headteacher, LEA 2*

This head went on to explain that when staff were asked to do returns on EAL learners, they had failed to list these boys:

The staff's perception was, this child does not want to be identified in a particular way, therefore I won't identify him. This child seems perfectly able, therefore they don't have a problem, why should they need any extra help? They didn't have a negative against the child. They actually had a very positive view of the child, but as a result, they weren't prepared to write the child's name down on a piece of paper and say this child is in my class. And that's all we were asking. Because in order to get support you have to identify how many students you have within your school. What I had to explain to people was, what we're saying here is, here is a student who could do better. You wouldn't in any other circumstances deny any child the opportunity to do better. Why should you do that in this particular child's case? And as I say, it was very much sensitivity about identifying students and believing that students did not want to be identified as different.

Under the previous and current frameworks inspectors are expected to report on the efficiency and effectiveness with which resources are managed, paying particular attention to the deployment of staff and other resources for pupils with EAL needs. One headteacher observed that inspectors had not asked any questions which would allow them to identify 'either positively, negatively or neutrally, any issue relating to ethnic diversity against performance indicators of any sort'. He pointed out that it wasn't a matter for discussion during the inspection, adding:

What the inspectors were saying is that there doesn't appear to be any issue arising from English as an additional language. Those children appear to be well integrated to different classes, taking part in classes, and did not appear to be excluded socially from group relationships in this school. ...It was couched in terms of 'well-integrated', 'participating' and 'making progress', as opposed to any resource provision for those children. ...Because there isn't any additional sort of provision for them. Because the thresholds are quite low, because of our numbers. Some of them are, yes, in the earlier stages of language acquisition, but the majority, of course, have got language acquisition, but maybe not on the same level as their peers here. *Primary headteacher, LEA 2*

This observation matches our analysis of inspection reports. It would appear that inspectors generally tend not to comment on the actual attainment or progress of children with EAL but are making rather general statements about social integration. In this school which has relatively few children with EAL, no additional resources were claimed or allocated to them. But this was not considered to be an issue by the inspectors commenting on the management of resources.

White schools and race equality

We were particularly interested to understand how schools that had few students from ethnic minorities, or those which were exclusively white in their pupil composition, perceived equality issues. An LEA officer argued that the new inspection framework and guidance needed to be strengthened to support such schools:

> My feeling is that the OFSTED work should be able to encompass white schools. It's obviously as important or more important for schools in white areas to prepare pupils to promote equalities and to promote awareness of pupils, an awareness that they may not have around them in the same way a [London] pupil does. You know pupils in [this LEA] are privileged to live in this sort of society because they meet people from different backgrounds all of the time, and if white pupils don't do that then you know, the school has to work harder. ...You know the recommendation that the Macpherson Report made, which was about curriculum reflecting cultural diversity, well the new curriculum doesn't quite go that far does it? And OFSTED don't go that far either. If OFSTED did now, I think that would encourage those white schools to go further. *LEA officer*

A primary headteacher explained how she understood her role as regards race equality in a predominantly white school:

> I think, actually, in schools like this, [where] there is a smaller percentage of children who come from ethnic minority groups, that you have to make a specific decision to include... The curriculum content has to in-

clude things from other cultures, so that you do bring in the children who are in the minority. ... I mean, I was going to say you don't get perhaps so many issues to do with bullying, but then you may have found something completely different. I mean, I used to work in the inner city in L where there was a much higher percentage of children from ethnic minority groups in the school and you know the white population accepted them, I felt, fairly readily. I feel that here, on the odd occasion, we have had children where it is obvious that their parents are racially prejudiced and they have given their children those views. And therefore, because we haven't had such a high proportion of children from those groups in the school, they would then become the victim, more readily so, of bullying, We obviously have to make sure that if we do hear of any of those kind of incidents we act very, very strongly among those groups. *Primary headteacher, LEA 3*

Another headteacher also argued that multi-ethnic schools were advantaged over white schools:

I think that [the situation of predominantly white schools] is an important issue that sometimes is not taken seriously enough. I think [this school] has a built in advantage. It's in a multi-ethnic community, a community that has for a long time been multi-ethnic, so there's a sense that the people who live here, have always lived here reasonably well together and so the multi-ethnicity of the community is always there. That is its natural state. I mean there's a school in the south of [the borough], which is a white school, in which there's been a sort of trickling of black pupils into the school. It's a white school, a white working class area, National Front, all those sort of thing have been there. Now they are getting a lot of refugees because they are under-subscribed and therefore the issues for them are much more difficult to cope with than the issues for us. They are starting from a very different point and I think that any sort of inspection process would have to recognise that, recognise that there is the sort of racism which is long gone here. *Secondary headteacher, LEA 1*

It is not just in white working class areas that the local community can include individuals and groups with racist views. One headteacher of a primary school in LEA 3 spoke of the racism which was 'endemic' among the white middle class parents of her pupils, which needed to be positively countered in school. As we have argued in chapter two, the OFSTED framework and guidance gives little support to race equality issues in predominantly white schools. OFSTED's application of the term 'educational inclusion' (OFSTED, 2000) ignores racism as a feature of school or society which may operate to exclude. (See the section in chapter two entitled *Educational inclusion and race equality* for a discussion of this). The section below, entitled *Racial tension,* highlights an example of a school where racism in the local community and school has been ignored for several years. In this case racial violence and the threat of such violence are now undermining the students' security at school and their opportunities for learning.

Race and the community

> I still feel the one thing that OFSTED [misses] ... We as a school feel about OFSTED is that we know we need to engage with our ethnic communities. We only just appointed our first Afro-Caribbean parent governor. I think that it's important that we get the views of our ethnic minorities, both parents and students. *Secondary headteacher, LEA 2*

While acknowledging that OFSTED inspection processes do engage parents and pupils to some degree, this headteacher felt that the efforts his school was making to develop an effective partnership with parents from minority communities was insufficiently recognised, in both the OFSTED framework and the processes of inspection.

Another headteacher recognised that she had to learn more about provision for equality within the changing local community. But she did not know where to turn for advice, since her situation and experiences were likely to be very different from those in inner city schools where the percentage of ethnic minority pupils was much higher than in her school:

> As the school changes, as [the area] changes, I'm trying to learn about it. And it's, I think there are some tricky problems. Because, you know, one of the things [with] Pakistani families is this business of children disappearing for six months to go back to Pakistan just when they should be doing some GCSE coursework. And then the parents wondering why they don't do very well in the school system and that's a really difficult issue to handle, because I can't say to them that the school's system is going to bend to their needs. *Secondary headteacher, LEA 2*

Other headteachers were conscious that they needed to take account of past and present discrimination experienced by families and communities when developing partnerships with parents from minority communities. As one primary head expressed it:

> I am well aware that the parents of some of the children from non-white racial backgrounds, may have experienced in their own upbringing within this country, a range of abuse, or have a range of experiences and some of them may not be that positive. So I feel that I have got a responsibility to them as parents, that they would want something different for their children and I want that too, I wouldn't want that sort of cycle to be repeated. *Primary headteacher, LEA 2*

Headteachers were highlighting for us some of the challenges they face and acknowledging that they needed additional support, advice and training. Challenges were not restricted to those working in multi-ethnic or changing communities. Headteachers who worked with white communities also identified race equality issues as among their responsibilities:

> You could actually walk into a school like this and see a lot of white faces and think there would be no problems. And I am not sure that is the case. In fact, quite the reverse, because among some of the older villagers here it [race] would be a bigger issue. So, we are very conscious as a school, in fact there is something going on at the moment where someone was called a racial name. That may have been an incident in another school with a larger mix, and might not even have warranted a mention to a member of staff. But in a school like this we actually do stress that this is unacceptable and we do have pupils telling us what's going on and we do act, hopefully, appropriately, on each particular case. *Secondary headteacher, LEA 3*

Racial tension

We have seen how, in a predominantly white community, the need for strategies to address and prevent racism may not be easily recognised by all. In one of the schools we visited, the headteacher pointed out that the OFSTED inspection report had commented favourably on racial harmony when, in fact, there were, and continue to be, considerable tensions between local white and Bangladeshi residents. These tensions are also felt within the school community. Around twelve per cent of the pupil population is of Bangladeshi descent and the remainder largely white.

The headteacher explained that these tensions have existed over many years – they were being reported in the local press at the time of our visit. The school serves a community where around sixteen per cent of young men are unemployed and where nearly half the adult population does not have access to a car. This is in a relatively prosperous town where people in most other neighbourhoods enjoy full employment. The headteacher had been appointed after the OFSTED inspection. He explained:

> We are looking at our policies [on equalities] and we have done a lot of work with the local community and the police as well. All of this to try and deal with an issue that I have certainly been aware of for fourteen years and has been getting worse, but which hasn't really been tackled head-on in the school before and wasn't raised as an issue by OFSTED. *Secondary headteacher, LEA 2*

Assaults on pupils on the way home from school had necessitated a police presence outside the school each afternoon, and students had been involved in rival gang violence at lunch time. Gangs had come onto the school site and assaulted students. At the time of the OFSTED inspection, members of the local community evidently decided to cover up these problems. The head explained:

> I was told about the inspection here that the students, and parents for that matter, pulled together because they regarded it very much as their school on their estate and no inspector was going to try and come around causing trouble. *Secondary headteacher, LEA 2*

Apparently, then, it was possible for a school to gain a favourable OFSTED report despite racial tensions in the school and community, which continue to have serious impact on learning and on all aspects of the school's provision. These problems were effectively hidden from the OFSTED inspection team at the pre-inspection parents' evening and during interviews with students. The inclusion of an explicit question on equality in the parental questionnaire might usefully provide inspectors with another source of evidence to enable them more accurately to judge whether there is racial harmony in the school and community or racial tension.

Can race equality be inspected?

Some members of HMI have expressed doubt about whether the Macpherson recommendation that OFSTED monitor the implementation of strategies to prevent and address racism in schools, can be fully realised (see chapter three). Given that this recommendation has been accepted by Government, and is a key OFSTED responsibility, we asked headteachers whether they felt the OFSTED framework and processes of inspection would permit such monitoring and how they would feel about being monitored in this way. All felt that inspection had a key role to play and, with some reservations, they welcomed the idea that OFSTED inspection should monitor schools' efforts to address and prevent racism. One difficulty acknowledged was that OFSTED inspections can only provide a 'snapshot' picture of a school and that equalities initiatives are likely to be ongoing:

> In terms of 'this is best practice', I think that sometimes that is a bit more difficult because I am not sure that in a snapshot OFSTED evidence gathering over four days, you can actually make a judgement of something like ... racial practices. ...I think your evidence base may be more complicated and therefore one needs to talk to parents, one needs to talk to children individually. ...A lot of OFSTED is about a snapshot. It is about hard data gathering. A lot of other things are impressionistic and they are subjective, so I think yes they could make some remarks about whether they have seen certain things or not. But then to go from that to making hard-nosed judgements might be much more difficult. *Primary headteacher, LEA 2*

Another headteacher felt that OFSTED should be inspecting race equality and that schools need to be accountable in this area as in others. She did, however, stress that OFSTED inspectors need to recognise that such work is sometimes difficult and that it needs to be part of a whole school approach to working with children and their families:

> I am not against them doing it [inspecting how schools are preventing and addressing racism]. I think that it has got a place in the inspection because the inspectors will come in and look at a whole range of things and that is very important and if there are problems then they should be picked up during that week. There is no doubt about that, because who else will pick them up? If the head and the school aren't doing

something then that should be something that they [inspectors] should look at. I think that one of my views is ... that they should be looking at the whole way in which the school is encouraging all pupils to behave towards each other. Because sometimes if you are trying to deal with prejudice, you are focusing a lot upon a particular racial group and there could be a question of prejudice being more entrenched if the parents at home aren't supporting. ...What I am trying to say is, fundamental to [challenging] any kind of prejudice must be a whole policy on how pupils behave towards each other anyway. *Primary headteacher, LEA 3*

The opinion expressed above by this headteacher of a village primary school was shared by the headteacher of a multiracial secondary school in London:

The OFSTED inspection process has a key role to play in diagnosing that the schools are doing what they should be. And there are now some very clear things. I mean you need to have a policy. That policy should bite across the school. ... There has to be clear things about statistical evidence of how pupils are doing in schools and looking at outcomes. And I think that OFSTED should go in within its framework and look at schools to ensure that those things are in place. And I suppose, if they're not in place and they are put in place, then OFSTED has promoted an equalities agenda within the school. The problem with equalities, is that unlike target setting and assessment, which you can do quite coldly, ...with equalities you have to have an understanding of it or it can go quite badly wrong. You have to know what it means. You can't just assume that the school is going to have a good equalities policy because you are told that it should have one and that if next time it's inspected if it doesn't, it's in trouble. There are very complex issues around prejudice and institutional racism that probably go further than just telling someone that something has got to be in place. ...I think the problem with the OFSTED inspection process itself is that it's impossible for it to be a subtle process in a sense. *Secondary headteacher, LEA 1*

This headteacher went on to argue that if OFSTED made a critical assessment that identified race equality initiatives as a priority for a school, that school would need support and expertise from the LEA in order to address and prevent racism. We have noted in this chapter how this was successfully accomplished in a village primary school in LEA 3, which developed a curriculum which reflects cultural diversity in response to an inspection assessment which highlighted this as a key action point.

Another headteacher, who believed that the OFSTED framework was, in principle, generally robust enough to address and prevent racism in school, pointed out that the inspection process needed to be linked to the processes of self-evaluation in a school:

> If someone tells you your practice is good then that reinforces your best. If they criticise that shouldn't prevent. ...I don't think we can be dependent upon OFSTED. What we are dependent upon, in a way, is OFSTED coming in and auditing what we are doing to make sure things are right. It's a four yearly or six yearly stamp of approval. So yeah, I think it is a means [of monitoring strategies to address and prevent racism]. I don't think anybody will ever take away inspection because it's a useful device in terms of saying it's all right. But, I mean, increasingly self-evaluation of the school becomes easier and easier because of the tools you can now use. *Secondary headteacher, LEA 2*

The political context of inspection

As the quotation that opens this chapter indicates, headteachers in our sample were very aware of the political context in which schools are expected to challenge racism and promote race equality. One headteacher pointed out that inspection is not only serving a number of purposes but that inspection reports also have a number of different audiences:

> In one sense it is serving a straightforward political process, it is saying that we as a Government are committed to the raising of standards in whatever areas, so it is serving a political purpose. We are telling you, the voters, that we are hard-nosed, we are reaching out, we are doing things. Secondly, it is attempting to inform the professionals in the school of issues that they should carry forward, should make improvements in and, as I said earlier, if you are lucky, it could give you some pointers to help you on your way so that you are not wasting your time. So it is a professional tool. Thirdly, it is also public reporting. Now those three do not always lie easily together. And in providing a professional tool to enable the school to make improvements, sometimes I think governments feel that that will only happen if what is in the public's domain is the stick to beat the school. And it may well be, but on the other hand,

it may actually, depending on the sophistication of the evidence gathering and the reporting itself, not aid that in the way the report then goes out to the community at large. It could actually be quite destructive to a community which is seeking to improve. It is getting the balance between the two and making the decision whether an OFSTED inspection can fulfil three goals and sometimes it may be quite difficult to do that. *Primary headteacher, LEA 2*

We recognise the sensitivity which such reporting requires, and we note the training implications for contracted inspectors. The headteacher quoted here was suggesting that race equality issues should be explicit in the everyday work of schools, so that the Government's agenda on race equality becomes a regular part of educational discourse and practice rather than something hidden in broad references to social or educational inclusion. He continued:

I wouldn't like to think that we are talking about sweeping things [such as race equality] under the carpet. ... One of the things I think with race relations and social development requires, is the chance for people to reflect as opposed to making immediate responses. ...I think that sometimes an ill-timed report and maybe an ill-phrased report, or maybe one which is simply abused by others mischievously, can undermine the progress that an institution might be making. *Primary headteacher, LEA 2*

The above quotation and the first one of the chapter come from primary headteachers, working in predominantly white middle class communities. They are willing to take on the challenges of the Macpherson report, to prevent and address racism in schools. Another headteacher, in the same LEA but based in a working class and more culturally diverse school community, was also struggling to promote race equality. He expressed the need for support from both politicians and agencies such as OFSTED in confirming this agenda and pointed out that:

If race equality is a Government priority in education no one has made it clear to me. *Secondary headteacher, LEA 2*

Summary

The headteachers in our study were all broadly sympathetic to the notion that OFSTED inspection should include the monitoring of strategies to address and prevent racism in school. They recognised that this could be achieved within the current framework, but that inspectors would need to be carefully briefed and trained if they are to accomplish this sensitive task in an appropriate profession manner. Schools which receive critical assessments would need support from LEA advisers to enable them to address any weaknesses. Some head-teachers also acknowledged the need for their own further training in this area. This was most notable in LEA 2, a new unitary authority in the south of England, and in LEA 3, a Midlands shire county.

Doubts are sometimes expressed as to whether 'middle England' is ready to accept initiatives which address race equality. Indeed, some members of HMI question whether schools in predominantly white communities are ready to take forward such initiatives (see chapter three). LEA 2 and LEA 3 both share many of the characteristics of what is sometimes characterised as 'middle England'. LEA 2, for example, encompassed, in 1997, key Labour marginal constituencies that had been previously been represented by Conservative Members of Parliament. Both local MPs are now Labour. All the headteachers in our sample in both the London borough and in LEAs 2 and 3 wish to promote race equality in their schools. Many are looking to OFSTED and to Government to offer leadership in this field.

Chapter 7

CONCLUSIONS AND RECOMMENDATIONS

We set out to investigate how OFSTED is fulfilling the responsibilities given to it by Government in March 1999 to monitor strategies in schools to prevent and address racism. During the period of our research, OFSTED introduced a new inspection framework in January 2000. The timing of our research allowed us not only to examine inspection reports written under the previous framework but also to discuss with HMI, contracted inspectors, and headteachers whether the new framework is likely to prove a more effective evaluative tool for monitoring race equality.

OFSTED and its responsibilities in preventing and addressing racism

We discovered that OFSTED has not yet informed either schools or contracted inspectors of its lead responsibility to monitor strategies to prevent and address racism in schools. Nevertheless, the new inspection framework is a potentially powerful tool for carrying out this role. It is designed to encourage inspectors to write reports which are less descriptive and more evaluative. Like the previous framework, it requires inspectors to talk to pupils and to parents in order to collect data on the quality of education provided. Although parents and carers are issued with a questionnaire which invites them to comment on the school's provision and invites them also to make judgements about the management of the school, it does not ask them any questions about any aspect of equality, including race equality.

The current inspection framework has a number of additional features which have the potential to contribute to greater racial equality in schools. It adopts the term 'educational inclusion' to cover a range of equality issues, including race equality. Yet this document fails to discuss racism or its impact on learners, whether these learners are from minority or majority ethnic communities.

The notion of 'educational inclusion' is to underpin training for contracted inspectors, although the timetable for this training has yet to be confirmed and it is not yet certain whether it will be mandatory. Evidence from our interviews suggests that race equality is not yet recognised as central feature of educational inclusion by all at OFSTED.

Unfortunately the new framework does not require schools to systematically monitor pupils' attainment and achievements by ethnicity. It is these processes of ethnic monitoring which would reveal any differentials between groups in attainment, in access to the school's services and provisions, and in the use of disciplinary procedures such as exclusion. There are also some uncertainties within HMI as to whether regular school inspection is capable of revealing evidence of racial harassment and bullying, which is something that the Government requires OFSTED to monitor.

Members of OFSTED recognise the need for 'a common language' when discussing issues of race equality. Yet some HMIs, including some members of the OFSTED senior management team, themselves lack confidence in using such a language. We argue that race equality has yet to become a central part of the corporate culture and discourse within OFSTED.

Inspectors' perspectives

Contracted inspectors were agreed that both the former and the current inspection frameworks permit the inspection of race equality issues in schools. They argued that the degree to which such issues are to be found in reports depends, firstly, on the sensitivity of individual contracted inspectors to such issues and, secondly, on the degree of importance which the reporting inspector as team leader attaches to race equality. Although the former inspection schedule provided a common framework for reporting on race equality and other equalities issues, lack of experience and/or expertise among contracted inspectors meant that, in practice, the benefits of such a common framework were often lost to schools.

Inspectors argued that they needed specific training on race equality issues if they were to be effective in this area. They were also of the opinion that schools needed training on race equality and, in particular, on the value and importance of ethnic monitoring as part of their efforts to improve the quality of education and overall educational standards.

Inspectors recognised the importance of EAL provision, but were concerned that it was often designated to someone who lacked the specific skills and expertise to make accurate judgements of EAL provision, based on the evidence. In particular, concerns were expressed about the quality of reporting in schools where the numbers of pupils needing such provision were small.

It was generally recognised by inspectors and headteachers that race equality issues in white schools were of considerable importance. Inspectors believed that such schools needed further guidance from OFSTED on this aspect of their provision.

The section of the inspection framework which addresses pupils' spiritual, moral, social and cultural development is generally recognised by inspectors as the part of the inspection framework where provision for race equality, and particularly cultural diversity, might be inspected. A number of concerns were raised, however. These related to the extent to which this aspect of the framework might encourage inspectors to view pupils from ethnic minority communities as presenting attitudinal or behavioural problems to schools. Inspectors believed that associating race equality primarily with the spiritual, moral, social and cultural development of pupils distracted from two key issues. The first is the need to ensure high standards for all pupils, regardless of ethnicity, and the second is the need for schools themselves to make structural changes in order to guarantee equality of access to all the school has to offer.

Inspectors recognised that the collection of evidence on racial harassment and bullying was difficult within the constraints of the inspection time-scale and resources. This concern was shared by a member of HMI we interviewed.

Inspectors also recognised that the effectiveness of a school's provision in promoting race equality and addressing racism was likely to depend on the leadership of the headteacher.

It was generally believed by contracted inspectors that inadequacies in a school's provision for race equality were not likely to lead to a judgement that a school is failing or in need of special measures.

Contracted inspectors were not convinced that the OFSTED leadership recognised race equality as an essential feature of quality in education. They looked to its leadership actively to support them in developing this aspect of educational and social inclusion. Headteachers also looked to OFSTED and to Government to provide stronger leadership in this field.

Inspection reports

We examined in detail 30 reports completed under the previous inspection framework. The inspection reports tended to follow a standard format. The language used in the overall judgements rarely prioritised issues of race or addressed attainment by specific ethnic groups. Although differentials in attainment were identified in the text of some reports, the tendency was for such issues to become hidden in stock phrases like 'the need to raise improvement for all' or the need for improved recognition of 'cultural diversity' in a school's curriculum.

The term race equality was absent from reports. Our findings were supported by OFSTED's own text search for the term race equality. In 10,623 reports between 1997 and 1999, race equality or racial equality is found in only 0.25 per cent of the reports. In relation to the reports examined, the concerns central to this research were implicit rather than explicit. Race equality was generally marginal and often wholly absent.

Data on ethnicity was inconsistently applied. Critically, precise numerical data on the ethnic composition of pupil populations were missing. Where ethnic data were used, this was most frequently to define the characteristics of a school and its catchment area, rather than to consider pupils' attainment, achievements or progress. It was difficult to establish the extent to which a school, or its curriculum, matched the needs of its pupils.

The needs of pupils with English as an additional language were not always addressed coherently. The distinction between pupils with special educational needs and those for whom English is an additional language was not always clear. In the absence of precise evidence from the inspection reports, it is difficult for a reader to establish the extent to which sufficient and appropriate EAL support is being given. It is also difficult to assess the impact of a school's provision on pupils' performance.

Headteachers' perceptions

Prior to inspection, headteachers in our sample did not generally anticipate that equality issues in general, or race equality in particular, were likely to be a feature of inspection. The headteachers felt that while OFSTED should monitor the strategies used to address and prevent racism in schools, this will only be done sensitively and professionally if contracted inspectors are given appropriate training. For schools to be able to act on any negative assessments they will need follow-up support and advice from external advisers, particularly from their local education authority advisory services.

Interviews with headteachers indicate that not all recognise the value of ethnic monitoring of pupils' attainments and achievements. Some headteachers do not recognise that monitoring by ethnicity is an important tool which can support the processes of target setting. A number of the headteachers in our sample acknowledged that they need training and support if they are to challenge inequalities effectively and address and prevent racism through education.

Can race equality be inspected?

Inspection is only one means by which provision for race equality in schools can be monitored. For schools to develop as inclusive and just communities they will also need to engage in processes of self-evaluation and monitoring. Inspection is, nevertheless, a key tool, and the Government has entrusted OFSTED with a lead responsibility in monitoring how schools are addressing and preventing racism. It is important that OFSTED and its inspectors are publicly accountable in relation to race equality and cultural diversity issues. HMCI's Annual

Report, other thematic reports by OFSTED and those on individual schools have the potential to enhance race equality in education. It is important that the impact of inspection processes and reports on race equality is systematically and independently evaluated.

7. Recommendations
To the Department for Education and Employment

- Provide detailed guidance to schools on the purposes and practicalities of monitoring pupils' attainment and achievements by ethnicity, as a key aspect of improving standards in schools

- Require and resource schools to introduce ethnic monitoring within a specified time-scale and to respond to any inequalities in attainment and provision it identifies

- Require and facilitate the ethnic monitoring of teacher employment

- Publicise to schools OFSTED's Government-designated lead responsibility for monitoring strategies to address and prevent racism in schools

- Ensure that LEAs are provided with appropriate resources to follow up and support schools which receive critical assessments of their provision for race equality

- Resource training for headteachers on race equality issues, giving priority to the needs of both the headteachers in schools which are experiencing changes in their ethnic composition (for example, the enrolment of refugees and asylum seekers) and to those who work in predominantly white communities

- Establish an independent, publicly accountable working group to evaluate the 'impact of inspection' processes and reporting on race equality in education.

To OFSTED

- Publicise to contracted inspectors and the wider educational community OFSTED's designated lead responsibility for monitoring strategies to address and prevent racism in schools

- Encourage a corporate culture and discourse of race equality within OFSTED

- Recognise and promote race equality as a central feature of the drive to improve standards in schools

- Require schools to systematically monitor their provision by ethnicity, including pupil attainment and the school's use of sanctions such as exclusion

- Expand OFSTED's definition of educational inclusion in the context of inspection to address how all learners, and particularly learners in predominantly white schools, might be encouraged to challenge racism and promote race equality

- Routinely include a comment on issues of race equality in that part of the school inspection reports sent to parents

- Provide guidance to inspectors and headteachers on indicators of race equality in schools, including indicators in predominantly white schools

- Provide guidance to inspectors and schools on ethnic monitoring as an essential feature of school inspection and school self-evaluation

- Ensure that training for contracted inspectors on educational inclusion is mandatory

- Ensure that race equality is an explicit feature of mandatory training for contracted inspectors

- Enhance inspector training on race equality with regular instructions and guidance, made available on the OFSTED web-site and in regular OFSTED publications such as *Update*

- Ensure that all inspectors required to inspect EAL provision are given appropriate training

- Amend the pre-inspection parents' questionnaire to include an assessment of equalities initiatives in general and provision for race equality in particular

155

- Where appropriate, invite parents to comment on a school's EAL provision

- Review whether regular school inspections are, in practice, an effective means of monitoring schools' strategies to prevent racial harassment and bullying and, if not, arrange for a special HMI inspection of this provision

- Ensure that race equality issues are given priority in early reviews of the new inspection framework and in reviews of contracted inspectors' reports

- Conduct or commission further research on how OFSTED might most effectively monitor strategies to prevent and address racism in schools

- Require inspectors to identify in their reports successful strategies adopted by schools to promote race equality

- Require inspectors to establish whether those attending the pre-inspection parents' meeting are representative of the school population in terms of ethnicity

- Require inspectors to provide interpretation services wherever this is appropriate to ensure parents' full participation in pre-inspection meetings

To schools

- Develop self-evaluation tools on race equality

- Encourage dialogue between teachers, parents and governors on ways of promoting race equality in the school

- Engage in discussion with OFSTED inspectors about race equality initiatives and the self-evaluation tools the school has developed, viewing inspection as an additional opportunity for professional dialogue

- Use and apply the CRE Standards for Racial Equality in Schools, *Learning for All* (CRE 1999)

References

Audit Commission (1999) *Missing Out: LEA management of school attendance and exclusion*. London: Audit Commission.

Centre for Public Policy and Practice (1999) *The OFSTED System of School Inspection: an independent evaluation*. Uxbridge: CEPPP.

Commission for Racial Equality (1999) *Learning for All: standards for racial equality in schools*. London: CRE.

Department for Education and Employment (1999) *Social Inclusion: pupil support*. London: DfEE.

Doherty, G.D. (ed) (1994) *Developing Quality Systems in Education*. London: Routledge.

European Commission (1997) *Accomplishing Europe through Education and Training: report of the Study Group on Education and Training*. Luxembourg: Office for Official Publications of the European Communities.

Fidler, B., Earley, P. and Ouston, J. (eds) (1996) *Improvement through Inspection? Complementary approaches to school development*. London: David Fulton.

Fitzgibbon, C.T. and Stephenson, N.J. (1999) 'Is inspection helpful?' in (ed) C.Cullingford *An Inspector Calls*. London: Kogan Page, pp 97-118

Gillborn, D. and Gipps, C. (1996) *Recent Research on the Achievements of Ethnic Minority Pupils*. London: HMSO.

Home Office (1996) *Racial Tensions and Harassment in Schools: a report of the Racial Attacks Group* London: Home Office

Home Office (1999) *Stephen Lawrence Inquiry: Home Secretary's Action Plan*. London: Home Office.

Home Office (2000) *Stephen Lawrence Inquiry: Home Secretary's Action Plan, first annual report on progress*. London: Home Office.

Hopkins, D., Harris, A., Watling, R. and Beresford, J. (1999) 'From Inspection to School Improvement?' Evaluation of the Accelerated Inspection Programme in Waltham Forest'. In *British Educational Research Journal*, 25(5): 679-690.

MacBeath, J. (1999) *Schools Must Speak for Themselves*. London: Routledge.

Macdonald, I., Bhavnani, R., Khan, L. and John, G. (1989) *Murder in the Playground: the report of the Macdonald Inquiry into racism and racial violence in Manchester schools*, The Burnage Report. London: Longsight.

Macpherson, W. et al (1999) *The Stephen Lawrence Inquiry*. Report of an Inquiry by Sir William Macpherson. London: The Stationery Office.

Maychell, K. and Pathak, S. (1997) *Planning for Action*. Slough: NFER.

Millett, A. and Johnson, D.C. (1998) 'OFSTED Inspection of Primary Mathematics: are there new insights to be gained?' In *School Leadership and Management*, 18(2): 239-255.

Office for Standards in Education (1995) *Framework for the Inspection of Schools.* London: The Stationery Office.

Office for Standards in Education (1996) *Exclusions from Secondary Schools 1995/6.* London: The Stationery Office

Office for Standards in Education (1999a) *Handbook for Inspecting Primary and Nursery Schools.* London: The Stationery Office.

Office for Standards in Education (1999b) *Handbook for Inspecting Secondary Schools.* London: The Stationery Office.

Office for Standards in Education (1999c) *Handbook for Inspecting Special Schools and Pupil Referral Units.* London: The Stationery Office.

Office for Standards in Education (1999d) *Inspecting Schools: the framework.* London: The Stationery Office.

Office for Standards in Education (1999e) *Inspecting Subjects and Aspects 11-18 Equal Opportunities.* London: OFSTED, February.

Office for Standards in Education and Training (1999f) *Inspecting Subjects and Aspects 11-18 English as an Additional Language*, London: OFSTED, February.

Office for Standards in Education and Training (1999g) *Raising the Attainment of Minority Ethnic Pupils: school and LEA responses.* London: OFSTED Publications Centre, March.

Office for Standards in Education and Training (1999h) *OFSTED Inspection Forms*, London: The Stationery Office on CD-ROM.

Office for Standards in Education and Training (1999i) *PICSI Annex for Primary Schools.* London, OFSTED, Summer Version 1.

Office for Standards in Education (2000a) *The Annual Report of Her Majesty's Chief Inspector of Schools 1998-99.* London: The Stationery Office.

Office for Standards in Education (2000b) *Educational Inclusion and School Inspection.* London: OFSTED, Inspection Quality Division.

Office for Standards in Education (2000c) *Update.* No. 32, Spring.

Osler, A. (1997) *The Education and Careers of Black Teachers: changing identities, changing lives.* Buckingham: Open University Press.

Osler, A. (1999) 'Citizenship, democracy and political literacy'. In *Multicultural Teaching,* 18 (1): 12-15 and 29.

Osler, A. (2000a) 'Children's rights, responsibilities and understandings of school discipline'. In *Research Papers in Education,* 15 (1), 49-67.

Osler, A. (2000b) 'The Crick Report: difference, equality and racial justice'. In *The Curriculum Journal,* 11 (1): 25-37.

Osler, A. and Hill, J. (1999) 'Exclusion from School and Racial Equality: an examination of government proposals in the light of recent research evidence'. In *Cambridge Journal of Education,* 29(1): 33-62.

Osler, A. and Starkey, H. (1996) *Teacher Education and Human Rights.* London: David Fulton.

Ouseley, H. (2000) 'The Stephen Lawrence effect'. In *Multicultural Teaching,* 18 (2), 18-20.

Ouston, J.P., Earley, P. and Fidler, B. (1996) *OFSTED Inspection: the early experience.* London: David Fulton

Ponchaud, B. (1997) 'OFSTED Inspection Findings: a tool for self-evaluation?'. In *School Science Review,* 79 (September): 17-20.

Qualifications and Curriculum Authority (1999) *The National Curriculum for England.* London: QCA.

Richardson, R. (1994) Equality Assurance and the Inspection of Schools: a study of 50 of the first 56 reports to be published, with particular attention to how they treat the theory and practice of equality of opportunity. A report for the Runnymede Trust, June.

Richardson, R. and Wood. A. for ROTA (1999) *Inclusive Schools, Inclusive Society: race and identity on the agenda.* Stoke-on-Trent: Trentham.

Sentamu, J. (2000) 'Valuing cultural diversity in education'. In *Education Futures: lifelong learning,* RSA/ Design Council.

Social Exclusion Unit (1998) *Truancy and School Exclusion.* London: Cabinet Office.

Troyna, B. and Hatcher, R. (1992) *Racism in Children's Lives: a study of a mainly white primary school.* London: Routledge.

Watling, R. (2000) *OFSTED school inspections and school self-evaluation: A review of published research and policy on behalf of the NASUW.* University of Leicester: Centre for Citizenship Studies in Education.

Wilcox, B. and Gray, J. (1995) 'The Inspection Model: the views of LEA Chief Inspectors'. In *Cambridge Journal of Education,* 25(1):63-74.

Wright, C. (1992a) Early Education: multicultural primary school classrooms. In D. Gill, B. Mayor, and M. Blair (eds.) *Racism and Education: structures and strategies.* London: Sage.

Wright, C. (1999b) *Race Relations in the Primary School.* London: David Fulton.

INTERVIEW SCHEDULE: INSPECTORS

Race Equality and OFSTED inspection
INTERVIEW SCHEDULE
INSPECTORS

Introduction
Purpose of research
Permission to tape record: issues of anonymity and confidentiality
Permission to use data for research purposes

Request background information on interviewee. Experience as inspector, and in which roles as team member

Q1 In what ways does the current inspection and reporting framework support the goal of race equality?

Q2 To what extent is there a common framework for reporting on race equality issues and how is this shared among the team?

Q3 To what extent does the framework include the use of the school's ethnic monitoring procedures for making judgements that inform the main findings? (PROBE: what happens when information is unavailable or incomplete?)

Introduce the following questions, indicating that they will follow the current framework as found in inspectors' reports

Characteristics of the school

Q4 In what circumstances do you record the ethnic make-up of a school among its characteristics?

Curriculum

Q5 What curriculum developments would you be looking for to support race equality?

Q6 Would you please explain the processes involved in collecting and analysing curriculum based evidence that supports race equality?

Q7 What sort of provision for pupils with English as an Additional Language would you expect to see in a successful school?

Q8 What do you consider to be good race equality indicators in schools that are predominantly white? (PROBE: distinctions from/similarities with indicators in schools with above average ethnic minority composition)

Pupils' spiritual, moral, social and cultural development

Q9 What kind of indicators demonstrate evidence of pupils' moral, social, and cultural development, and how are they linked to race equality?

Q10 To what extent do you consider explicit reference to race equality an important element of anti-bullying policies in *all* schools?

Leadership and Management in Schools

Q11 What do you consider to be the role of the heads/senior managers/ and governors in race equality initiatives?

Q12 How might management practices further support race equality?

Educational standards, monitoring and evaluation

Q13 What school policies would you expect to see in place that support the goals of race equality, and how would you judge the policy in practice/action?

Q14 How might initiatives to improve educational standards and pupil performance support the goal of race equality?

Relationships with parents and the community

Q15 In what ways do judgements about relationships with parents and the community support the goals of race equality?

Staffing and staff training

Q16 What staffing measures might, in your view, enhance race equality? (PROBE: staff training as an indicator for race equality)

Q16 Do you consider that staffing matters are given sufficient weighting in inspection reports?

Schools in special measures/with serious weaknesses

Q17 Are there issues of race equality/inequality which might cause a school to be designated as having serious weakness/be in need of special measures? If so, how are these identified?

Summary questions and ways forward

Q18 In your experience, are OFSTED teams well equipped to advise schools on matters of race equality, and to what extent are schools able to understand and act on the advice given?

Q19 Does the formula of reporting on 'best' and 'worst' practice help in the achieving of race equality goals?

Q20 Finally, how would you interpret the role of inspection to support race equality as found in the recent Home Office Plan (following the Stephen Lawrence Inquiry), and to what extent do you consider that the inspection and reporting framework might be extended to further promote race equality?

INTERVIEW SCHEDULE: HEADTEACHERS

Race Equality and OFSTED Inspection
INTERVIEW SCHEDULE
HEADTEACHERS

Introductions

Purpose of research – link to focal points 3 and 4 of the research viz

3. the study addresses the extent to which inspected schools have understood assessment in inspection reports of race equality issues

4. the study considers the extent to which the current *Framework*, in particular its emphasis on a general reporting of best and worst practice, supports or inhibits the reporting of race equality outcomes, and the effects of that reporting upon subsequent school-based developments

Permission to tape record: issues of anonymity and confidentiality
Permission to use data for research purposes

Request background information on school.

Inspection processes

Q1 When was your school last inspected? When is the next inspection due (if known)?

Q2 Prior to the most recent inspection in the school, to what extent and in what ways were you made aware that issues of equality of opportunity and, in particular, issues of racial equality, were inspection issues? (PROBE: how was this known – from pre-inspection visit, from documentation, from process itself...)

Q3 To what extent are/were all staff aware of race equality as a feature of inspection and of the degree of importance attached to it by inspectors?

Q4 Were you aware of the kinds of evidence that OFSTED inspectors would/will consider to be useful race equality indicators?

Q5 What do *you* consider to be useful indicators of race equality in your school, and how are they similar/different to those considered by OFSTED (if known)?

Q6 In what ways does the school keep records of ethnic composition, to what extent, and how was such data used by the inspection team to inform the main findings?

Q7 To what extent were you made aware of EAL as an area of inspection interest?

Inspection outcomes – the report and follow up

Q8 Following the inspection process, to what extent and in what ways was the inspection report helpful in enabling the school to pursue/extend developments as they relate to race equality?

Q9 In terms of school-based practice, how important is/was it to have an inspection report that included equality issues (and/or issues of race equality) and how confident did the school feel about acting upon report recommendations?

Eliciting headteachers' views on matter of race equality

Q10 What curriculum developments in the school do you consider to support the goals of race equality?

Q11 What developments in the area of pupils' spiritual, social, cultural and moral development do you look for in the school to support race equality, and how is this identified and monitored?

Q12 How important do you see your role and that of senior management in supporting race equality? (PROBE: examples of management policy and practice)

Summary questions and ways forward

Q13 In your experience, are OFSTED teams well equipped to advise schools on matters of race equality, and to what extent are schools able to understand and act on the advice given?

Q14 Does the formula of reporting on 'best' and 'worst' practice help in the achieving of race equality goals?

Q15 Finally, how would you interpret the role of inspection to support race equality as found in the recent Home Office Plan (following the Stephen Lawrence Inquiry), and to what extent do you consider that the inspection and reporting framework might be extended to further promote race equality?

APPENDIX ITEM 3

CORRESPONDENCE BETWEEN AUDREY OSLER AND HMCI, CHRIS WOODHEAD

Our Ref. AHO/SEH

CONFIDENTIAL

Mr. Chris Woodhead
Her Majesty's Chief Inspector
OfSTED
Alexandra House
33 Kingsway
London WC2B 6SE

School of Education

21 University Road
Leicester LE1 7RF · UK
Tel: +44 (0)116 252 3688
Fax: +44 (0)116 252 3653

Director
Tom Whiteside

18 February, 2000

Dear Mr. Woodhead,

CRE Research Project: OfSTED School Inspection and Race Equality

We have now interviewed a number of your staff as part of the above project. I would like to clarify a number of points in relation to the data we have collected.

1. It would appear from the interviews that some HMI were not aware of the key role assigned to OfSTED in the Government's response to the Stephen Lawrence Inquiry. Are you able to provide us with any documents which draw the attention of HMI to the role of OfSTED School Inspection in the Home Secretary's Action Plan?

2. The Home Secretary's Action Plan states that: 'OfSTED …. will ensure that the important issues raised in the report are addressed during inspections'. May we have a copy of any letter/memorandum that has been sent to HMI, registered inspectors or headteachers concerning this?

3. We were informed by one of our senior OfSTED respondents that within OfSTED: 'Race equality is not a priority. Our priority is under-achieving white boys'. I would appreciate your response to this.

Interviews with OfSTED personnel have proved a very rich source of data and we appreciate the time that your staff have given us. However, I am anxious to clarify the above issues directly with you since you were unable to meet us to discuss OfSTED and race equality in person.

Thank you for your consideration of these questions. I look forward to your reply.

Yours sincerely,

Professor Audrey Osler

cc. Phil Barnett, CRE
Dr. Marlene Morrison

Alexandra House
33 Kingsway
London WC2B 6SE

Tel 0171-421 6800 (Switchboard)

Fax 0171-421 6546 GTN-3066

Chris Woodhead
Her Majesty's
Chief Inspector of Schools

26 MAR 2000

OFFICE FOR STANDARDS
IN EDUCATION

Professor Audrey Osler
University of Leicester
School of Education
21 University Road
Leicester LE1 7RF

1 March 2000

Dear Prof. Osler,

I am replying to your letter of 18 February.

We do not rely on paper communication in OFSTED. Important issues are always a matter for discussion in division meetings.

The new inspection Framework and Handbook, which have been given to you already, provide stronger guidance on all inclusion aspects including race-related issues. All independent inspectors will undergo further training in this area of inspection. The enclosed booklet summarises and reinforces the guidance in the Handbooks.

I am, frankly, surprised by the statement allegedly made to you that 'our priority is underachieving white boys'. Our priority is underachievement, full stop.

Yours sincerely,

CHRIS WOODHEAD

APPENDIX ITEM 4
AN INSPECTION FRAMEWORK FOR RACE EQUALITY AND SOCIAL JUSTICE

Questions

Each of the following questions addresses aspects of the relation between the inspection framework and issues of equality and social justice

■ **Characteristics of the school**
What kind of school is this?

Do reports contain adequate descriptions of the school's composition in terms of pupils' attainment on entry, gender, ethnicity, and background?

■ **Attainment and progress**
What are its educational standards?

Is performance data analysed by stages and by comparison with national averages and similar schools?

Do reports indicate whether the attainment and progress of minority groups is comparable with others?

Are performance data analysed in relation to different groups of pupils?

Are differences/similarities indicated on the basis of ethnicity and/or gender?

How well are students taught?

How do teaching approaches relate to the needs of different groups of pupils?

■ **Attitudes, behaviour, and personal development**
How well does the school take care of its pupils?

Does the inspection framework evaluate and report on pupils' responses to teaching and other provision made by the school, as shown by the quality of relationships in the school, including the degree of racial harmony?

Do reports make judgements about how well students relate to one another, including relations among and between different ethnic groups?

Do inspection reports provide evidence of inappropriate behaviour, including racial harassment and bullying?

Do inspection reports note the level of respect between pupils and teachers and other adults in the school, and whether pupils are encouraged to articulate their own beliefs and views?

Do inspectors report on the extent to which pupils are interested in views and ideas that are different to their own, and whether pupils understand a diversity of beliefs, attitudes, and social and cultural traditions?

■ **Teaching**
Do the reports highlight the extent to which teaching meets the needs of all pupils?

What focus is there upon pupils with EAL?

■ **Curriculum and assessment**
In what ways do inspection reports evaluate and report on the planning and content of the curriculum and the extent to which its contribution to the educational standards achieved by all pupils?

In what ways do reports evaluate how curriculum planning and implementation takes account of age, capacity, ethnicity, background, and competence in teaching EAL and SEN?

Do the inspection reports evaluate procedures for assessing pupil attainment?

Do inspectors report on the equality of access provided by the curriculum and the opportunity for pupils to make progress?

Do reports consider the impact of pupil organisation into class and teaching groups upon the equality of access and opportunity?

Do reports make judgements about the effectiveness of careers guidance?

■ **Pupils' spiritual, moral, social and cultural development**
Do reports evaluate and report on pupils' spiritual, moral, social and cultural development, through the curriculum and life of the school, and through the example set for pupils by adults in the school?

Do reports evaluate collective worship?

Does the inspection framework allow for the reporting of the ways in which schools provide pupils with knowledge and understanding of values and beliefs and enables them to reflect upon their experiences to promote spiritual awareness and self-knowledge?

Do the reports indicate whether schools teach principles to distinguish between right and wrong?

Do reports include the extent to which pupils are encouraged to respond positively to one another?

Do the reports provide evidence of the extent to which pupils are encouraged to take responsibility, participate fully in the school community, and develop an understanding of citizenship?

Do reports make judgements about the extent to which pupils are taught to appreciate their own cultural traditions and the diversity and richness of other cultures?

Is diversity seen as a cause for celebration? Is bilingualism among pupils seen as a cause for celebration?

■ **Support, guidance, pupils' welfare**
Do reports evaluate provision for pupils' educational and personal guidance, and its links to educational standards achieved?

Does inspection report on and evaluate the effectiveness of measures to eliminate oppressive behaviour including all forms of racial harassment and bullying?

Do reports note the systems by which bullying and harassment are recorded, and the steps taken to prevent repetition?

■ **Partnerships with parents and the community**
Do reports present evidence about the effectiveness of a school's partnership with parents?

Do the reports examine the extent to which schools are maximising opportunities to gain the involvement of parents?

Do reports make judgements about the schools' relationships with the community?

■ **Leadership and management**
To what extent do reports evaluate the role of headteacher, staff, and governing bodies in contributing to the quality of education and standards achieved by all pupils?

To what extent is the term 'positive ethos' linked to the quality of school leadership and management?

What attention is given to 'equal opportunities in the reporting of leadership and effective management?

■ **Staffing, accommodation and learning resources**
Do reports refer to and report on the adequacy of staffing, accommodation and learning resources?

To what extent do inspector teams report on the quality of teacher and support staff who work with pupils with EAL?

■ **Efficiency**
To what extent do reports provide evidence of the efficiency and effectiveness with which resources are managed?

APPENDIX ITEM 5

OFSTED JUDGEMENT RECORDING FORM: SCHOOLS

JUDGEMENT RECORDING FORM: SCHOOL

PART A: GRADES FOR SCHOOL CHARACTERISTICS, STANDARDS, QUALITY AND MANAGEMENT

Grade 1 - 7 or 0 (insufficient evidence) with, as appropriate:

Grade 1	Excellent			
Grade 2	Very good	Favourable	Well above average	Promotes very high standards and quality
Grade 3	Good			
Grade 4	Satisfactory	Broadly Typical	Average	Promotes sound standards and quality
Grade 5	Unsatisfactory			
Grade 6	Poor	Unfavourable	Well below average	Promotes very low standards and quality
Grade 7	Very poor			

		U5s	KS1	KS2	KS3	KS4	Post-16	School
1	SCHOOL IMPROVEMENT							
1.1	Improvement since last inspection							4
1.2	Capacity for improvement							3
3	SCHOOL CHARACTERISTICS							
3.1.1	Attainment on entry							4
3.1.2	Socio-economic circumstances							3
4	EDUCATIONAL STANDARDS ACHIEVED							
4.1.1	Attainment				3	3	3	3
4.1.1.1	Attainment in English				3	3		3
4.1.1.2	Attainment in mathematics				2	3		3
4.1.1.3	Attainment in science				3	3		3
4.1.2	Progress				3	3	3	3
4.1.3	Progress of pupils with SEN				3	3	0	3
4.2.1	Attitudes							3
4.2.2	Behaviour							3
4.2.3	Relationships							2
4.2.4	Personal development							2
4.3	Attendance							3
5	QUALITY OF EDUCATION							
5.1	Teaching				3	3	3	3
5.2	The curriculum				3	3	3	3
5X	Assessment				3	2	2	2
5.3	Provision for pupils' SMSC development							2
5.4	Support, guidance and pupils' welfare							3
5.5	Partnership with parents and the community							2
6	MANAGEMENT AND EFFICIENCY							
6.1	Leadership and management							2
6.2	Staffing, accommodation and learning resources							3
6.3	Efficiency							3
6.4	Value for money							3

Is there reported evidence of significant variations in any of the following?

Enter   *Y for Yes*
           N for No
           0 for insufficient evidence to form a view.

		Y,N,0
P1	Attainment or progress of girls and boys (Framework 4.1)	Y
P2	Attainment or progress of different ethnic groups (4.1)	O
P3	Test/examination results over time (4.1)	N
P4	Progress of pupils of differing attainment (4.1)	N

Is there reported evidence of non-compliance with any of the following statutory requirements (where applicable)?

Enter   *Y for Yes*
           N for No
           Z for not applicable.

		Y,N,Z
P5	The National Curriculum (Framework 5.2)	N
P6	Religious education for all pupils, other than those withdrawn by parents (5.2)	Y
P7	Sex education (5.2)	N
P8	Daily collective worship for all pupils, other than those withdrawn by parents (5.3)	Y
P9	Health and safety requirements (6.1)	N
P10	Any other statutory requirement (6.1)	N

175

PART B: GRADES FOR INDIVIDUAL STRENGTHS AND WEAKNESSES WITHIN PROVISION AND MANAGEMENT

Grade 1 - 7 or 0 (insufficient evidence) with, as appropriate:

Grade 1	Excellent		
Grade 2	Very Good	A significant strength	Promotes very high standards and quality
Grade 3	Good		
Grade 4	Satisfactory	Neither a particular strength nor weakness	Promotes sound standards and quality
Grade 5	Unsatisfactory		
Grade 6	Poor	A serious weakness	Promotes very low standards and quality
Grade 7	Very Poor		

5 QUALITY OF EDUCATION PROVIDED

Grades 1 – 7

		U5s	KS1	KS2	KS3	KS4	Post-16
5.1	TEACHING						
5.1.1	Teachers' knowledge and understanding				3	3	3
5.1.2	Teachers' expectations				3	3	3
5.1.3	Teachers' planning				3	3	3
5.1.4	Methods and organisation				3	3	3
5.1.5	Management of pupils				3	3	3
5.1.6	Use of time and resources				3	3	3
5.1.7	Quality and use of day-to-day assessment				3	3	3
5.1.8	Use of homework				4	4	3

		U5s	KS1	KS2	KS3	KS4	Post-16
5.2	CURRICULUM						
5.2.9	Breadth, balance, relevance of the whole curriculum				3	4	3
5.2.10	Equality of access and opportunity				3	3	3
5.2.11	Provision for pupils with special educational needs				3	3	0
5.2.12	Planning for progression and continuity				3	3	3

		School
5.2.13	Provision for extra-curricular activities, including sport	1
5.2.14	Careers education and guidance (secondary schools only)	3

		U5s	KS1	KS2	KS3	KS4	Post-16
	ASSESSMENT						
5.2.15	Procedures for assessing pupils' attainment				2	2	2
5.2.16	Use of assessment to inform curriculum planning				3	3	2

		School
	LITERACY AND NUMERACY	
5.2.17	Effectiveness of the school's strategy for literacy (primary schools only)	
5.2.18	Effectiveness of the school's strategy for numeracy (primary schools only)	

		School
5.3	SPIRITUAL, MORAL, SOCIAL AND CULTURAL DEVELOPMENT	
5.3.1	Provision for pupils' spiritual development	3
5.3.2	Provision for pupils' moral development	2
5.3.3	Provision for pupils' social development	2
5.3.4	Provision for pupils' cultural development	2

THE MANAGEMENT AND EFFICIENCY OF THE SCHOOL

		School
5.1	LEADERSHIP AND MANAGEMENT	
5.1.1	Leadership: clear educational direction for the school	2
5.1.2	Support and monitoring of teaching and curriculum development	4
5.1.3	Implementation of the school's aims, values and policies	2
5.1.4	Development planning, monitoring and evaluation	2
5.1.5	The school's ethos	2

		School
5.2	STAFFING, ACCOMMODATION AND LEARNING RESOURCES	
5.2.6	Match of number, qualifications and experience of teachers to the demands of the curriculum	2
5.2.7	Match of number, qualifications and experience of support staff to the demands of the curriculum	3
5.2.8	Arrangements for professional development of all staff	1
5.2.9	Adequacy of accommodation for effective delivery of the curriculum	4
5.2.10	Adequacy of resources (inc books/materials/equipment) for effective delivery of the curriculum	3

		School
5.3	EFFICIENCY OF THE SCHOOL	
5.3.11	Financial planning	3
5.3.12	Use of teaching and support staff	2
5.3.13	Use of learning resources and accommodation	4
5.3.14	Efficiency of financial control and school administration	2

		School
X	ISSUES SPECIFIED BY HMCI (notified separately)	
a	....	
b	....	
c	....	
d	....	
e	....	

177

Grade 1-7

		School
5.4	SUPPORT, GUIDANCE AND PUPILS' WELFARE	
5.4.5	Procedures for monitoring progress and personal development	4
5.4.6	Procedures for monitoring and promoting discipline and good behaviour	2
5.4.7	Procedures for monitoring and promoting good attendance	3
5.4.8	Procedures for child protection and promoting pupils' wellbeing, health and safety	2

		School
5.5	PARTNERSHIP WITH PARENTS AND THE COMMUNITY	
5.5.9	Quality of information for parents	2
5.5.10	Parental involvement in children's learning	3
5.5.11	Enrichment through links with community	1

TEXT SEARCH IN BRS DATA BASE

(Supplied by Research Department, OFSTED, December 1999)

Text Search in BRS database

No of inspection reports in BRS database

1997-98	6,154
1998-99	4,469
1997-99	10,623

Search Term	1997-98		1998-99		Grand Total 1997-99	
	No of hits	% of total documents	No of hits	% of total documents	No of hits	% of total documents
Racial equality	9	0.15	10	0.22	19	0.18
Race equality	2	0.03	5	0.11	7	0.07
Racism	272	4.42	331	7.41	603	5.68
Harassment	1033	16.79	785	17.57	1818	17.11
Racial harassment	110	1.79	98	2.19	208	1.96
Bullying	4709	76.52	3699	82.77	8408	79.15
Gender equality	11	0.18	9	0.20	20	0.19
Linguistic equality	0	0	0	0	0	0
Bilingualism	17	0.28	15	0.34	32	0.30
Bilingual	499	8.11	418	9.35	917	8.63
English as an add language	1676	27.23	2142	47.93	3818	35.94
EAL	137	2.23	100	2.24	237	2.23

INDEX

NOTE: page numbers in italics refer to figures.

achievement *see* attainment
and achievement;
standards
anti-racism, 25
see also racism
attainment and achievement
concepts of, 49-50
of EAL pupils, 136-8
of ethnic minority pupils,
16, 28, 43-4, 75, 108-9,
122, 132-4
statistics on, 108-9
see also standards

behavioural issues
exclusions, 14-15, 20, 21,
33, 117-18
framework references to,
29
report references to, 119-
20
bilingualism *see* EAL
bullying *see* racial harassment
and bullying

Commission for Racial
Equality (CRE), 1
community
links with schools, 48, 81-
2, 120-1, 140-2
racism and racial tension
in, 57-8, 139-40, 141-2
CRE (Commission for Racial
Equality), 1
cultural knowledge and
development
framework references to,
29-30, 31
HMCI Report, 17-18
inspectors' views, xx, 78-
9, 151

report references to, 111-
14
curriculum
framework references to,
30, 34, 45
HMCI Report, 17
HMI views, 45
inspectors' views, 75-6
report references to, 111-
14, 123
see also personal development

DfEE (Department for
Education and
Employment)
race equality guidelines,
15
recommendations to,
xxiii-xxiv, 154
document analysis, 3, 8-9, 91-
2

EAL (English as an additional
language)
and attainment, 136-8
conflated with EO, 51, 53
conflated with SEN, 115,
123, 153
headteachers' views, 135-
8
HMCI Report, 16
HMI views, 45-6
in-class support and
withdrawal, 116
inspectors responsible for,
36, 46, 95, 135-6
inspectors' views, xx, 76-
7, 151
and national averages, 98
PICSI data on ethnicity
and, 97-8

report references to, xxii,
105, 106-7, 114-17, 123,
124, 153
Education Reform Act (1988),
4
educational inclusion
HMI views, xviii, 49-52
inspector training on, 20-
1, 62-4
in OFSTED framework, xvii,
21-7, 150
see also race equality
*Educational Inclusion and
School Inspection*, 22-3,
26
EMAG (Ethnic Minority
Achievement Grant), 13,
14
English as an additional
language *see* EAL
equal opportunities (EO)
conflated with EAL, 51,
53
inspector responsible for,
95
OFSTED language of, 61
report references to, 110,
122
statutory requirements, 35
equality issues
framework approaches to,
70
see also race equality
ethnic composition of
inspectors and HMIs, 54-
5, [U]94[u]
ethnic composition of schools,
xxii, 103-4, 105, 122, 135
Ethnic Minority Achievement
Grant (EMAG), 13, 14

ethnic minority pupils
classified as 'problem', 98-9, 106
data on attainment, 16, 28, 43-4, 75, 108-9, 122, 132-4
HMCI Report references to, 14-19
socio-economic circumstances, 98-9
see also EAL; racial harassment and bullying
ethnic monitoring
and educational inclusion, 22-3
framework guidelines, xviii-xix, 28, 33, 42-4, 150
headteachers' views, xxiii, 131-2, 134-5, 153
HMCI Report, 16
HMI views, xviii-xix, 42-4, 68
inspectors' views, 73-5
training in, 74-5
see also ethnic composition of schools
ethnicity, PICSI data on EAL and, 97-8
exclusions, 14-15, 20, 21, 33, 117-18

failing (underachieving) schools, xxi, 6, 18-19, 55, 82-3

Gillborn, D., 5
Gipps, C., 5
Government
approach to race equality, 5-6, 11-12
see also Home Office Action Plan

harassment see racial harassment and bullying
headteachers
interviews with, 127
perspectives, xxii-xxiii, 153
ethnic monitoring, target setting and standards, xxiii, 131-5, 153

inspectability of race equality, 143-5
inspection of EAL, 135-8
OFSTED role in preventing racism, 143-5, 146-7
political context of inspection, 145-6
race and community, 140-2
race equality and inspection agenda, 127-31
white schools and race equality, 138-40
support and training for, xxiii, 140-1, 146, 147
see also school management
HMCI (Her Majesty's Chief Inspector of Schools), 59
HMCI Report (1998-99), 13-20
HMI (Her Majesty's Inspectorate)
ethnic composition of, 94
interviews with, 39-40
perspectives
current and former frameworks, 40-9
curriculum, 45
educational inclusion, xviii, 49-52
ethnic monitoring, xviii-xix, 42-4, 68
inspection processes, 52-5
monitoring EAL, 45-6
OFSTED's role in preventing racism, 58-67
parents and community, 48
race equality in education, 56-8
race equality language, xix, 60-2, 63-4
racial harassment, 46-8
training and awareness raising, 62-4
review of inspection reports, 52

training for, 65-6
see also inspectors
Home Office Action Plan (1999), 5-6, 12-13
Home Office Report (1996), 5

inclusion see educational inclusion
inequalities, report references to, 123
inspection frameworks, xvii-xviii, 5
context of current, 11-12
and race equality, 27-8, 124-5
curriculum issues, [U]30[u], 34, 45
EAL monitoring, 45-6
educational inclusion, xvii, 21-7, 150
ethnic monitoring, xviii-xix, 28, 33, 42-4, 150
fitness for purpose, 89-90
HMI views, 40-9
inspectors' views, xix, 69-71, 73
parent and community links, 32, 35, 48
potential of current, 149-50
pupil care issues, 31, 34-5
racial harassment, 46-8
school descriptions, 28, 29
school management, 32, 35
standards issues, 28, 29-30, 33-4
teaching issues, 30, 34
inspection handbooks, 36-8
inspection reporting, 53-4
inspection reports, xxi-xxii, 121-4, 152-3
description of school, 42-3, 53-4, 73-5, 103-7, 135
ethnic data, xxii, 103-4, 105, 122, 152
guidelines for see inspection frameworks
HMI review of, 52

key issues for action, 109, 115, 130-1
language and format, 110, 121-2
for parents, 36
references to curriculum, 111-14, 123
references to EAL, xxii, 105, 106-7, 114-17, 123, 124, 153
references to EO, 110, 122
references to harassment, bullying and racism, 111, 119, 123-4
references to inequalities, 123
references to pupil care, 117-20
references to race equality, xxii, 92, 109, 110, 122, 152
references to school, parent and community links, 120-1
references to staffing, 123
references to standards, 108-11
review and analysis of, 7-9, 102
statistical data in, 122
inspection team documents, 96-7
inspections
agenda regarding race equality, 127-31
guidelines for *see* inspection frameworks
headteachers' views *see* headteachers
HMI views on processes of, 52-5
inspectability of race equality, 87-8, 143-5, 153-4
political context of, 145-6
pre-inspection data transformed during, 99, *100-2*

race equality in context of, 5
research on, 88-91
short inspections, 53
inspector-focused evidence, 3-4
inspectors
ethnic composition, 54-5, *94*
expertise and experience, 36
interviews with, 70
matched with schools, 54-5, 93, 95
perspectives
awareness of race equality, 71-2, 112
conflict avoidance, 72-3
curriculum issues, 75-6
EAL provision, xx, 76-7, 151
ethnic monitoring, 73-5
failing schools, xxi, 82-3
OFSTED's role, xxi, 83-5
overview, 150-2
parent and community links, 72, 81-2
pupils' personal development, xx, 78-9, 151
race equality and inspection framework, xix, 69-71, 73
racial harassment and bullying, xx, 79-80, 151
school leadership and staffing, 80-1
ways forward, 83-5
white schools, xx, 77-8, 151
Registered Inspectors, 72
Reporting Inspectors, 41, 71, 76
responsibility for EAL, 36, 46, 95, 135-6
responsibility for EO, 95
training, xix, xxiii, 7, 20, 66, 83

on educational inclusion, 20-1, 62-4
HMI views, 62-4
institutional racism, 23-7, 66-7, 80
interviews, 9
with headteachers, 127
with HMIs, 39-40
with inspectors, 70
'key issues for action', 109, 115, 130-1

Lawrence Inquiry report 5, 6, 11-12, 23-4
OFSTED response to, 7, 20-1, 67
leadership
inspectors' views of OFSTED, xxi, 83-5
see also Registered Inspectors; Reporting Inspectors; school management
LEAs (Local Education Authorities)
advice from, xxiii, 136, 144-5, 147
LEA-focused evidence, 4
policy role of, 4
recommendations regarding, 154
in research context, 7-8
literature review, 7-8, 88-91

Macpherson Report *see* Lawrence Inquiry Report
management *see* school management
matching
of inspectors and schools, 54-5, 93, 95
of pupils and teachers, 123
moral development *see* personal development
multi-agency collaboration, 81-2
multiculturalism, 17-18, 112, 114

national averages, 98
National Curriculum, 17, 26

O'Brien, Mike, 25
OFSTED (Office for
    Standards in Education)
    concept of educational
    inclusion, xvii, 21-7, 150
    inspection frameworks
    see inspection
    frameworks
    and language of race
    equality, 61, 68
    organizational culture,
    64-5
    recommendations to,
    xxiv-xxvi, 154-6
    role in preventing
    racism, xvii, xviii, 5, 12-
    13, 38, 149-50
        headteachers' views,
        143-5, 146-7
        HMI views, 58-67
        inspectors' views, xxi,
        83-5
        responses to Lawrence
        Inquiry Report, 7, 20-
        1, 67
        neglected in HMCI
        Report, 13-20
    views of race equality,
    67, 68
OFSTED documents
    Educational Inclusion
    and School Inspection,
    22-3, 26
    HMCI Report, 13-20
    Inspection Handbooks,
    36-8
    Raising the Attainment of
    Minority Ethnic Pupils,
    26, 90-1
    review and analysis of, 7,
    11
    standardisation in, 92
    see also inspection
    frameworks

parents
    inspection reports for, 36
    links with schools

framework references
    to, 32, 35, 48
    headteachers' views,
    140-1
    HMI views, 48
    inspectors' views, 72,
    81-2
    report references to,
    120
    pre-inspection data from,
    35, 96-7, 142, 149
personal development
    framework references to,
    29-30, 31, 34
    HMCI Report, 17-18
    inspectors' views, xx, 78-
    9, 151
PICSI (Pre-Inspection
    Context and School
    Indicator) data, 97-9
political context of
    inspection, 145-6
pre-inspection process, 33,
    35
    data transformed during
    inspection, 99, 100-2
    parents' meeting, 35, 96-
    7, 142, 149
    PICSI data, 97-9
pupils
    behavioural issues, 29,
    119-20
    exclusions, 14-15, 20,
    21, 33, 117-18
    matched with teachers,
    123
    see also ethnic minority
    pupils; personal
    development; racial
    harassment and bullying

QCA see National
    Curriculum
quality management, 88-9

race equality
    in context of inspections,
    5
    and educational
    inclusion, xvii, 21-7, 150
    evidence in schools of,
    52

Government approach to,
    5-6, 11-12
    headteachers' views see
    headteachers
    HMI views see HMI
    inspectability of, 87-8,
    143-5, 153-4
    and inspection
    frameworks see
    inspection frameworks
    and inspection
    handbooks, 36-8
    inspectors' avoidance of
    issues, 72-3
    inspectors' awareness of
    issues, 71-2, 112
    inspectors' views see
    inspectors
    language of, xix, 60-2,
    63-4, 150
    neglected in HMCI
    Report, 13-20
    OFSTED views, 67, 68
    report references to, xxii,
    92, 109, 110, 122, 152
    research on inspection
    and, 90-1
    in white schools, xx, 22,
    57-8, 77-8, 138-40, 151
racial harassment and
    bullying
    anti-bullying guidance,
    20, 21, 46, 124
    HMCI Report, 15-16
    HMI views, 46-8
    inspectors' views, xx, 79-
    80, 151
    report references to, 119,
    124
racial tension in
    communities, 141-2
racism
    Government approach to,
    11-12
    HMI views of, 57-8
    institutional racism, 23-
    7, 66-7, 80
    of pupils, parents and
    community, 57-8, 139-
    40, 141-2
    report references to, 111,
    123

role of OFSTED in preventing, xvii, xviii, 5, 12-13, 38, 149-50
  headteachers' views, 143-5, 146-7
  HMI views, 58-67
  inspectors' views, xxi, 83-5
  neglected in HMCI Report, 13-20
  response to Lawrence Inquiry Report, 7, 20-1, 67
  of staff, 133
Raising the Attainment of Minority Ethnic Pupils, 26, 90-1
recommendations
  to DfEE, xxiii-xxiv, 154
  to OFSTED, xxiv-xxvi, 154-6
  to schools, xxvi, 156
Registered Inspectors, 72
Reporting Inspectors, 41, 71, 76
research
  aims and objectives, xvi, 2-4
  context, xv-xvi, 4-7
  design and methodology, xvi, 7-9
  document analysis, 3, 8-9, 91-2
  evidence, 3-4
  literature review, 7-8, 88-91
  recommendations, xxiii-xxvi, 154-6
Richardson, R., 24-5, 90

school management
  framework references to, *32*, 35
  HMCI Report, 18
  HMI views, 51
  inspectors' views, 80-1
school-focused evidence, 4
schools
  described in reports, 42-3, 53-4, 73-5, 103-7, 135
    framework guidance, 28, *29*

ethnic composition, xxii, 103-4, 105, 122, 135
exclusions from, 14-15, 20, 21, 33, 117-18
inspectors matched with, 54-5, 93, 95
institutional racism, 23, 24-5, 80
links with community, 48, 81-2, 120-1, 140-2
links with parents [U]see[u] parents
multi-agency collaboration, 81-2
recommendations to, xxvi, 156
statistical data from, 95-6
statutory requirements regarding equality, 35
training for, 74, 83
see also failing schools; special schools; white schools
SEN (Special Educational Needs), 115, 123, 153
Sentamu, Dr. John, 25
short inspections, 53
significant, use of term, 110-11
social development *see* personal development
socio-economic circumstances, 98-9
Special Educational Needs *see* SEN
special measures, 6, 18-19, 55, 82-3
special schools, 18, 19, 37-8
spiritual development *see* personal development
staff
  racism of, 133
  see also teachers
staffing
  inspectors' views, 81
  report references to, 123
  standardisation, in OFSTED documents, 92
standards
  framework approach to, 28, *29-30*, 33-4

headteachers' views, 132-4
HMCI Report, 16
monitoring, 75
reporting on, 108-11
see also attainment and achievement
statistical data
  from schools, 95-6
  in inspection reports, 122
  on standards, 108-9
  see also ethnic composition; ethnic monitoring

target setting, 134, 135
teachers
  matched with pupils, 123
  see also staff; staffing
teaching, framework references to, *30*, 34
training
  in ethnic monitoring, 74-5
  for HMI, 65-6
  inspectors' views of, 83
  for inspectors, xix, xxiii, 7, 20, 66, 83
    on educational inclusion, 20-1, 62-4
    HMI views, 62-4
  for schools, 74, 83
  and support for headteachers, xxiii, 140-1, 146, 147
Travellers, 54, 72-3
truancy, 20, 21

underachieving schools *see* failing schools

white ethnicity, invisibility of, 105
white schools and race equality
  headteachers' views, 138-40
  HMI views, 57-8
  and inclusion, 22
  inspectors' views, xx, 77-8, 151
Wood, A., 24-5